Any good manager is in the communication business. A sure way for managers to fail is to stubbornly stick to their style and expect others to cater. Chris knows this. Communication with an entire generation has changed. Millennial motivations are different. Empowering this generation every single day is the currency that Chris understands. *The Millennial Whisperer* teaches skills to better communicate with Millennials that will make their work both meaningful and profitable.

BERT WEISS

TheBertShow.com Host, The Bert Show

The Millennial Whisperer should be required reading for every current or future business leader. The strategies Chris shares will not only help you better lead Millennials, but they will help you become a better leader for everyone.

JON GORDON

JonGordon.com

Author of 16 books, including six bestsellers: *The Energy Bus*, *The Carpenter*, *Training Camp*, *You Win in the Locker Room First*, *The Power of Positive Leadership*, and *The Power of a Positive Team*.

Millennials are hardworking and resourceful, two qualities that can take any company to new heights. *The Millennial Whisperer* will help you attract the right ones to your organization and set them up to succeed.

BEN KIRSHNER,

CEO, Elite SEM

Ranked as the #1 Best Workplace for Millennials

in the US by *Fortune* Magazine

The Millennial Whisperer is a must-read guidebook to the most-misunderstood generation. Learn more about your future leaders and uncover tactical ways to turn Millennials into your secret weapon.

JEREMY GUTSCHE

CEO of TrendHunter.com and New York Times bestselling author of *Better and Faster: The Proven Path to Unstoppable Ideas*

Nothing is as significant as the generational changes we are undergoing. Tuff does a great job of outlining some of the misunderstandings we have regarding the Millennial generation as well as tactical ways to turn them into our greatest assets.

STEVE KOONIN,

CEO Atlanta Hawks Basketball Club

The Millennial Whisperer does a great job summarizing and dumbing down complex generational issues into tactics that provide focus to get the best out of people. Tuff does this all while entertaining the reader—this is a must-read for all CEOs.

RAJ CHOUDHURY,

President, Brightwave

The Millennial Whisperer

THE MILLENNIAL WHISPERER™

THE PRACTICAL, PROFIT-FOCUSED PLAYBOOK FOR WORKING WITH AND MOTIVATING THE WORLD'S LARGEST GENERATION.

CHRIS TUFF

NEW YORK

LONDON • NASHVILLE • MELBOURNE • VANCOUVER

The Millennial Whisperer

The Practical, Profit-Focused Playbook for Working With and Motivating the World's Largest Generation

Published in New York, New York, by Morgan James Publishing. Morgan James is a trademark of Morgan James, LLC. www.MorganJamesPublishing.com

ISBN 9781642792775 paperback
ISBN 9781642792799 case laminate
ISBN 9781642792782 eBook
Library of Congress Control Number: 2018911126

Cover Design by:
John Stapleton

Interior Design by:
Chris Treccani
www.3dogcreative.net

Morgan James is a proud partner of Habitat for Humanity Peninsula and Greater Williamsburg. Partners in building since 2006.

Get involved today! Visit
MorganJamesPublishing.com/giving-back

DEDICATION

To my amazingly supportive wife, Julie, who cheered me along from the start. This is for you and wouldn't have been possible without you.

And to my daughters, Finley and Marlin, who inspire me to always see the greatness and beauty in life. My hope is the strategies in this book help create even better intergenerational experiences in the workforce that you get to benefit from someday.

And to Richard Ward, Brandon Murphy, David Rollo, Joel Lunenfeld, and Kris Pinto, five Millennial Whisperers who invested in me, showed me how to lead this amazing generation, and gave me the freedom to spread my wings and fly.

DISCLAIMERS

Throughout this book, I have tried to recreate events, locales, and conversations from my memories of them and independent research conducted. To maintain as much anonymity as possible, especially in circumstances where conversations were not always pleasant, I have changed names and identifying characteristics and details of people and places, such as physical properties, occupations, and places of residence.

This was done solely to permit me to share the *point* of the story used without unnecessarily revealing the *source* of the story.

Additionally, while I have made every effort to ensure that the information in this book was correct at press time, I do not assume and hereby disclaim any liability to any party for any loss, damage, or disruption caused by errors or omissions, whether such errors or omissions result from negligence, accident, or any other cause. No two circumstances are the same, so what worked in one organization or with one employee may not work in any other circumstance. You know your company, yourself, your prospects, and your employees better than anyone else. Thus, the information conveyed in here is solely for informational purposes.

Finally, while you'll see me reference 22squared throughout this book, the book is a production of The Millennial Whisperer, LLC, a Georgia limited liability company. I am a member and the Chief Executive Officer of The Millennial Whisperer, LLC.

Neither 22squared, Inc., nor any of its officers, agents, or employees has any relationship with the content of this book or The Millennial Whisperer, LLC. The only connection between 22squared and The

Millennial Whisperer, LLC is my being both a partner of the agency and a member and Chief Executive Officer of The Millennial Whisperer, LLC, a separate and independent entity.

TABLE OF CONTENTS

FOREWORD

Millennials are entitled, lazy, spoiled, self-absorbed, and disloyal employees—Period!

Are they? Really?

How do we attract, retain, empower, and lead Millennials?

This is one of the most pressing questions I am asked by business leaders from a personnel standpoint. It's one of the biggest challenges facing organizations today.

The idea of finding a productive Millennial is synonymous with finding the ever-elusive Loch Ness Monster, Bigfoot, or fire-breathing dragon. Have any of these Millennial myths crossed your path?

- They want immediate promotions after their first month on the job.
- They believe they are better at your profession than you are.
- They will quit the second they become upset.
- They are a me-first generation.
- They must have foosball tables, video games, and beer kegs in order to be productive.

Simply put, these myths are pure fallacy.

My man, Chris Tuff, the "Millennial Whisperer"

I recently facilitated an executive men's retreat. This retreat was specifically designed for high-level, success-driven, ambitious business leaders who are seeking purpose, significance, and fulfillment in life. It was a retreat where men could have true conversations about real life challenges in their careers, businesses, families, and lives. This was a place where successful men came to discover a more meaningful and balanced existence. Men who love the game of business are ambitious and under no circumstances will compromise their financial success. I built a safe and confidential space where men did the hard work and learned how to make courageous change in their lives while having fun during the process.

During this particular retreat, I met a rare force of nature named Chris Tuff. He continues to amaze me every day, and I know of no other way to describe this man. Sitting around a campfire, Chris spoke about his life experiences, challenges, tragedies, and triumphs as a husband, father, and business leader. Chris shared how he made courageous changes in his life and became a servant leader, motivator, and a true hero for his family, team, and advertising firm.

His team, all Millennials, showed true compassion for Chris's hard and courageous work to better himself. Not only did they understand where he'd been, but they also respected he'd bounced back in his life and career. Chris could see in his Millennial team their own appetite for change and betterment in their lives. They just needed someone to help them unlock their potential. They needed Chris Tuff, who became their mentor and ultimate champion.

Chris then discussed the bad reputation surrounding the Millennial generation and how he respected and loved working with his team. He cracked a joke about being a "Millennial Whisperer." I remember no one laughing. The group fell completely silent as Chris spoke about amazing experiences working with Millennials. He complimented not only their inspiring work ethic and motivation, but also the innovative ideas they bring to the table when empowered. These men listened intently to Chris discuss truths about Millennials they had never heard before.

I said to Chris, "You've got to write that book."

He said, "What book?"

"*The Millennial Whisperer.*"

Chris has created this powerful guide to get the most out of one of the greatest generations and workforces the business community has ever seen. Empowering and leading this generation will result in massive profits and increased productivity for leaders willing to implement the tactics outlined in *The Millennial Whisperer*. This book erases the myths and bridges the gap in communication between the Millennial generation and "us," the seasoned business executives they work with.

Throughout my career, from my professional beginnings at Deloitte, to coaching some of the top executives in the world, there is this false belief that the competition is for customers and market share. No! The competition is to attract the best and brightest workforce to our businesses. Financial success is dependent on empowering, leading, and retaining talent now and for a future of sustained success.

Happy People = Happy Customers = Happy Income and Cash Flow Statements.

And guess what, those people are the Millennials.

Great leaders such as Chris Tuff, Richard Branson, and Tony Hsieh have all realized this fact and are super successful as a result. What these trailblazers do differently is care deeply about their employees and empower their staffs to build a purpose-driven culture. This ultimately benefits customers and society at large.

It is our responsibility to inspire this generation, lead and encourage them, and then get out of their way! The return on investment in both time and money for those who implement the strategies in *The Millennial Whisperer* will be epic. *The Millennial Whisperer* teaches us how to:

- motivate and incentivize,
- have the difficult conversations, and
- attract, retain, manage, reward, and promote this powerful generation.

You now have two choices. First, continue doing what you have always done as a manager or leader of Millennials and ignore all of the wisdom in this book. Or, second, *take action*, implement Chris's tactics, and see the positive results unfold for your employees, time, and bottom line.

So many of us go through life searching for meaning and purpose. I believe Chris was born to be The Millennial Whisperer. It's his super power. I am truly humbled and honored to write this foreword because I believe this book is going to make a massive impact in business and, more importantly, people's lives.

I often say leaders listen first, ask questions second, respond, build trust, and make people feel safe and appreciated. In this book, Chris will show you how to be this type of hero leader for your Millennial team members.

One of my favorite mantras by Gay Hendrix from the book *The Big Leap* is, "I expand in abundance, love, and success every day as I inspire others to do the same."

Chris lives this mantra every day of his life and doesn't just talk the talk but walks the walk. His emotional intelligence along with the hard work he continues to do in his life, has created the great leader, man, husband, and inspiration Chris is today.

Take action, and you too will become a Millennial Whisperer!

Tommy Breedlove
TommyBreedlove.com
Featured Speaker, Writer, & Premiere Business & Life Coach
Proud Founder of the Choose Goodness movement

ACKNOWLEDGEMENTS

Thank you to everyone who helped make this book possible. A very special thank you to my editors, Nick Pavlidis, Sara Anna Powers, Jennifer Harshman, and Ethan Webb for helping me pull together all this content and make it shine. And thank you to my amazing sister, Sarah Tuff Dunn, who helped me define my voice and who at all hours of the day and night helped me find the right words to say when I could no longer find them.

Thank you to my amazing team of Millennials who were the inspiration for and subject of this book and who helped me find a new purpose in life. In no particular order, Raven Bennett, Shannan Farmer, Tyler Hartsook, Meg Roberts, Kiersten Smith, Mary Katherine Rordam, Ansley Williams, Casey Koppenhoefer, Leah Kircher, Caroline McMullan, Kevin Tyler, Samantha Pate, Daniella Capodilupo, Emily Grim, Mirian Romero, Mackenzie Lane, Kerry Abner, Lauren Bernath, and Sarah Jones.

To Brian Griffith, my favorite professor from Vanderbilt. Brian first taught me how to apply theory of organizations and people. He has now become a close friend and my checkpoint throughout the process of pulling this book together. Brian generously shared his course materials plus numerous studies about Millennials and the workplace. He's also the brains behind designing our Millennial Leadership Assessment and generously agreed to give readers of *The Millennial Whisperer* free access to take the self-assessment to find their strengths and areas requiring improvement when leading Millennials.

Thank you to Janis Middleton who helped me define the need and outline the importance for diversity and inclusion.

To John Stapleton who took my cover design and absolutely killed it with the different concepts and with the final product.

To Chris Gomersall who brought my website to life very early in this process.

To everyone who were my sounding board along the way—Alex Tuff, Ben West, Ese Sifo, Justin Epstein, Uloopi Fales, Justin Jones, Charlie Lively, and Quincy Jones. To my brother, Geoff Tuff, for sharing his wisdom and advice about writing and publishing. And to my mom, who helped raise me to be have both passion and (a bit of) patience, and my dad, who gave me a gene that determined I should write a book.

To my 22squared family who've been such an amazing group of colleagues and friends—Scott Sheinberg, Jenni McDonough, Genna Franconi, Mike Grindell, Carolyn Boyd, Barbara Jones, Curt Mueller, Kevin Botfeld, Mindy Adams, Anne Dinapoli, and Emilee Weaver.

To everyone who shared their amazing stories of being Millennial Whisperers with me—Ben Kirshner, Evan LaPointe, Marshall Mosher, Mike Hibbison, Chandler McCormack, Peter Boulden, Raj Choudhury, Sarah Bristow, Dave Williams, Robby Kukler, Meredith Guerriero, Joshua Backer, and Liza Nebel.

To Tommy Breedlove, who instigated this whole thing and picked me up when I was feeling down. And to the rest of the crew from The Exchange, Cody Hicks, and Trey Humphreys, who were all my support system from the very beginning to the last day of editing.

And thank you to my publisher, Morgan James Publishing, and the incredible team of David Hancock, Aubrey Kincaid, Jim Howard, Bethany Marshall, and I'm sure countless others who worked tirelessly behind the scenes and believed in this message enough to help me share it with the world.

This book would not be what it is without all of you. Thank you.

FREE MILLENNIAL LEADERSHIP ASSESSMENT

I'm a big believer in the old phrase, "what gets measured gets done." That's why I made sure this book is packed with practical, profit-focused strategies based on the best and latest research on leading Millennials in the workplace.

To that end, we partnered with G360 Talent Development to build a custom Millennial Leadership Assessment to allow you to analyze your strengths and identify areas for improvement in leading Millennials.

This powerful tool was developed by a team led by Dr. Brian Griffith, a professor, author, and former director of the Human and Organizational Development Program at Vanderbilt University.

And the good news is, every reader of *The Millennial Whisperer* can take the Millennial Leadership Assessment for free.

Before you read any further, I suggest taking the assessment to establish your baseline strengths and potential areas for improvement.

To claim your free Millennial Leadership Assessment, visit the book's Resources page at TheMillennialWhisperer.com/BookResources.

PREFACE

Ever heard of a passion disorder? Neither had I when my older brother Alex accused me of having such an affliction in 2011. At first, I thought perhaps he was referring to my feelings for my wife, Julie, about whom I've *always* been very passionate, so my reaction was to raise my eyebrows. What in the *what*?

I soon learned he was talking about my feelings for my *job*.

As leaders, we all have some level of passion disorder. That's often what makes us effective leaders. We love our companies, and we constantly look for better ways to do things. We look for better ways to serve our clients. We look for better ways to price our products and services. We look for better ways to motivate employees. We look for efficiencies and productivity strategies. So, I wasn't too offended when Alex accused me of having such a disorder myself.

I had spent most of my career working hard and proving people wrong. I'd constantly ask our CEO how high he wanted me to jump, and I'd jump much higher. I did whatever it took to get there—traveling the globe, networking until the party died, relentlessly pursuing new connections, and never *ever* giving up on a new lead.

It turns out, a passion disorder isn't *always* a good thing, though. It might be okay if kept at bay or in the short-term or to help push through during a time of struggle. But if that's your default level of intensity, it can consume even the strongest of leaders.

In 2016, I learned this the *hard way*.

I had been hired as the first real social media person at 22squared, a large advertising agency based in Atlanta. For years, I worked day and night to build out a successful social media practice. I had built a team and exceeded all expectations.

My team did so well, I was elevated to a partner, the youngest in the history of 22squared. From the outside, I appeared as if I had achieved something big and had everything going for me. But the weight and stress I felt were crippling.

I continued to work 24/7 and have my fingerprints on everything that had *anything* to do with social media. With hundreds of employees and social media marketing growing so big, I could barely keep up.

Still, by working harder and longer than any rational human being should, I kept going, setting sales records and achieving incredible results for our clients. After two more years, I started integrating the social media practice into a larger group at the agency, Media and Strategy, and was elevated again, this time to the EVP, Head of Business Development and Partnerships.

Everything seemed to be going well on the outside. But inside I was crumbling—and second-guessing everything I thought I knew about success. I had hit or achieved all expectations since 22squared brought me in to introduce social media marketing to the firm in 2008. I had exceeded all financial projections and built a team that was well respected in the market.

I kept questioning why I was struggling so much on the inside when I was achieving so much success. Why was I so stressed? Why was I always waiting for some other shoe to drop? How much more "success" would I need to achieve to feel better?

Admittedly, I didn't handle that pressure very well. I was drinking way too much. I was working way too hard. I was spending way too much time and energy on the wrong people. I had few "real" friends, and very few "real" relationships. I went out every night, networking, partying, doing everything I could to move up the corporate ladder and into the right social circles.

I spent way too little time at home, and way too little attention on my wife and two daughters. It was all work all the time (even if I was technically there, my iPhone was always in my hand).

Toward the end of 2016, I broke down. I couldn't handle the pressure anymore. There's no way success could feel so unfulfilling and stressful. Something had to give. At that point, I didn't feel like I had much left to lose. Work was overwhelming, and I wasn't taking care of myself. I was sick of pretending everything was okay, so I decided to take a month off to figure things out and get my head back on straight.

I didn't really have a plan beyond getting away for a while to isolate myself from work and my cell phone, figure out how to spend more time with my wife and daughters, and remove negative influences from my life.

Fortunately, my partners at 22squared fully supported my taking a month off. It had been obvious that I was struggling. (Apparently, I was the only person who fell for my "everything was okay" routine.)

Not many people knew *how bad* I had been struggling. But everyone knew I wasn't okay.

I did a lot of soul-searching that month.

You have to do that when you're an achiever committed to a month of unplugging from everything: my phone, my beers, my family. The tears? Yeah, there were two, or a few, or maybe more than a few.

That was the month my approach to *everything* shifted.

The iPhone that used to consume my attention became a simple tool.

I gave up drinking for good.

I recommitted to my family.

I redefined my metric of success. Making money would never again be my North Star. From then on, I started measuring my success based on making an *impact*—on my family, colleagues, and the world around me.

That simple shift in perspective made business fun again.

I was willing to let go of *anything* and *everything* that might draw me back to my old ways—including even leaving my successful career in advertising and the firm that had been my second home for nearly a decade if I had to.

Upon my return to work, I started another new position, this time leading the influencer marketing and content marketing teams that were helping companies attract attention through social media and building a broad online presence.

I also had a new group of team members to *lead—almost all of whom were Millennials.*

Yes, Millennials, that much-maligned generation born between 1981 and 1996 that's taking over the workforce. According to the Pew Research Center, in 2016 Millennials became the largest generation in the labor force, accounting for 35% of working Americans as of 2017.[1]

So there I was, fresh off a nervous breakdown, about to work with the people mocked as living in their parents' basements and playing video games.

What could possibly go wrong?

"*Greeeeeeeat,*" I thought. "Here we go."

But something amazing happened. My new attitude and determination to be a force for good in the marketplace connected really well with the unique perspectives Millennials brought to the table.

I also realized I had a newfound energy to lead. That month of elimination and perspective left me with so much more energy and focus for the things that mattered most. I channeled some of that newfound energy into managing this young team of Millennials—and they exceeded my expectations in nearly every conceivable way.

They worked harder and smarter than any people I had led before. They listened when I went on my passionate tirades on how change at our agency started with them. They brought new ideas, new inspiration, and new trends at a pace that I thought was impossible.

Work became fun again!

Their work ethic, attitude, and even production levels inspired me to become an even better and more effective leader than I had been before. So I resolved to become the type of leader I felt would really move the meter within our organization: an *empowering* leader.

With every passing day, they rewarded me with production and loyalty, crushing goals and all the key performance indicators we could throw at them. Yes, the Millennials.

It was almost as if the second I relinquished any desire to be perceived as the more traditional *hero* style of leader, it unleashed something powerful and almost unstoppable in them. You know—that guy who sweeps in and saves the day and solve all the problems in the workplace? That's the hero leader. That's who I tried to be for the first 13 years of my career. That's what almost took me out.

Instead, I made my Millennial employees the "heroes," and assumed the role of the "guide and coach." That caused me to shift to *equipping* them rather than trying to make them all clones of me.

And that made a massive difference in both our company culture *and* our profit levels.

They made me the hero in return—especially in the eyes of other leaders who had been leading the way I used to lead. They also taught me much more about leadership than the hundreds of experienced leaders and leadership gurus I had learned from since entering the business world.

I had found my solution to my burnout.

It had been right in front of me the whole time.

It was a small group of Millennials.

They helped me find the joy and fulfillment I'd been searching for in all the other places.

And they helped me achieve even greater success, personally and organizationally, only this time I actually felt the success.

I was also finally having the impact I desired—within my company, my city, and the world at large.

Whisper to Esteem

So, what will you find in this book? Well, one thing you *won't* find is theory. I've been in the business world for long enough to know that while theories look nice on paper, they don't do much good in the workplace.

Instead, you will find applied tactics—tactics *anyone* can use to get the most of the Millennials in the workplace.

You will also find strategies and stories from great leaders I've gotten to know and respect over the years, from dentists to ad-tech leaders, and everything in between. These leaders agree that, when managed in the right ways, the Millennial generation can unlock a whole new level of productivity.

You'll find tips for recruiting, retaining, and even promoting Millennials.

And the best part about these approaches is many of them are simple and small shifts that make a big impact. That means they can often be implemented *without a budget*. That's right. No budget necessary to get started. That also means you can try things without having to convene some high-level committee. You just start making your life better and business stronger while getting even more production from your team no matter what your title is at your company. You can get started right away.

I'll also share some strategies that are a little more involved but still doable for most companies and most leaders, especially as you build momentum and achieve positive results using the simpler strategies. I share these to make sure you have examples of tactics you can implement no matter where you are in the process of leading Millennials.

But *every* strategy is designed to generate a positive return on your investment of time and money, both to your sanity and to your bottom line.

I'll share not only the awesome insights I've learned by leaning into managing a team of Millennials but also insights from other leaders who are guiding Millennials successfully.

Millennials matter. They are both the present and the future of business. By 2030, they will be 75% of the American workforce (and 75% of customers, too. If we don't understand them, we can be sure our competitors will).

And by the end of our time together, you'll be able to leverage the power of Millennials to profit your own organization and impact the world for good.

Chris Tuff
a/k/a The Millennial Whisperer

DEBUNKING THE MILLENNIAL MYTHS

Recognizing That Millennials Have Been Misunderstood and Mismanaged

One of the easiest ways to take a worldwide cultural pulse about something is to type the term into Google but not hit enter. When you do, Google's autocomplete feature suggests a few options for you.[2] For example, when I type in "Cats are," Google's first four suggestions are that cats are "liquid," "evil," "better than dogs," and "jerks." Farther down the list are "awesome," "smarter than dogs," and "the best."

(Sorry, cat lovers, but I disagree with the last three, as does my English retriever, Tilly.)

According to Google, several factors such as other people's searches and trending stories go into the suggestions.[3] If you've already searched for something beginning with the term, Google will suggest your previous searches again.

So, what do you think people are searching when they start a search with "Millennials are"? Let me Google that for you, and feel free to Google it yourself. Just go to the main page and type in "Millennials are." To me, Google suggests "killing," "ruining," and "screwed," before I even hit Enter.

Killing seemed a bit harsh, but I was curious, so I continued typing to add *killing*. Google's next autocomplete suggestions included "the beer industry," "everything," "cable," and "relationships." People are obviously searching for "things" Millennials are perceived to be killing. A stereotype has run amok.

But this isn't a book about stereotypes. It's a book about reality. And the reality is, all these stereotypes are hurting businesses way more than they're hurting Millennials. And if we leaders focus on the stereotypes, we'll miss all the amazing things about Millennials. We'll work *against* them instead of locking arms *with* them to make our businesses more profitable, impactful, and enjoyable. So, let's start by addressing the reality of the stereotypes.

Truth in Numbers

Entitled, avocado-toast-eating, Ping-Pong playing, craft-beer-drinking, Game-of-Thrones-watching, unprepared, pessimistic slackers who are overly reliant on their parents—Millennials, right?

Wrong.

For seven years, Deloitte has been studying this demographic, with results that reveal the changing mindset. The Deloitte Millennial Survey 2018, which questioned more than 10,400 Millennials in 36 countries, found that 45% of respondents expect the economy to improve during the next year.

The data is clear. Millennials are actually working 45-plus hours per week, according to a study from ManpowerGroup. More than 20% of

Millennials are taking on side jobs, and 66% say they expect to work past 65; 12% say they have no plans to ever retire.

Hardworking, optimistic: that is the Millennial (who, yes, may enjoy avocado toast, but don't knock it till you try it). To really understand them, though, we need to dig a bit deeper.

Us and Them

First, let's consider a basic truth. Everyone has the potential to succeed given the right environment, a supportive culture, and key opportunities. Whether we are Sheryl Sandberg or Steve Jobs, we thrive in circumstances of curiosity, challenge, and control.

Millennials are, believe it or not, just like us—and then some. They're the most important group of people to any company's future success. They're the vast majority of workers and consumers. Ignoring or vilifying them will seal our fate.

Yet we continue to malign Millennials—in TV shows, in movies, and in any situation where the dreaded "M-word" comes up, and we roll our eyes. We, as leaders, peg Millennials as the most difficult generation to engage, retain, and manage. (If you don't believe me, check out "Millennial Job Interview" on YouTube, which has more than 5.6 million views as of this writing. Watch Amy, whose love of Pinterest, Starbucks, and Snapchatting with her boyfriend in Paris stun her potential employer—and herself.)

But what if we were wrong about Millennials this whole time? What if what we've experienced was more about *us* than it was about *them*? Leaders across the US and abroad have experienced the following:

- A shift in company morale when Millennials made an entrance
- Increased expectations for benefits the company should be providing
- Mounting tension between these new workers and the Boomers and Generation Xers who've been assigned to manage them

- Pushback on things such as dress codes, meetings, and flex time
- Rumblings, grumblings, demands for and expectations of promotions, quick pay raises, and bonuses

This happens in companies all over the place, big and small, and across industries. It's not unique to Millennials, either. Each successive generation has disrupted the workforce and our psyches: Baby Boomers, the "Video" Generation, the "Me" Generation, Generation X, Generation Y, and now Generation Z. As the *Atlantic* reports, it was around 500 BC when Socrates "swore the youth of his day loved luxury, displayed poor manners, and contradicted their parents and teachers."[4] In 1911, a letter to the same magazine "describes the rising generation as shallow, amusement-seeking, and selfish."[5]

Nature has a way of questioning change. (As the dad of two young daughters, I know this all too well.)

But it seems that Millennials are getting it even worse than previous generations did. Perhaps that's because there are more of them. Perhaps it's because social media spreads information faster than ever before. Whatever the reason, misconceptions about Millennials being lazy, entitled, or poor workers have tarnished this generation for years. They've also kept us from maximizing the potential of our Millennial workforce. That's all that they are, though: misconceptions. We must replace the misconceptions with practical, actionable, and *profitable* strategies for leading this new generation; and our businesses can be bigger, better, and *easier to lead* than ever before.

Second, take a look at what has changed during the Millennials' lifespan. Millennials—especially the older ones—have experienced a previously unheard-of amount of change in a tiny time frame—and during their formative years, to boot. In elementary school, they used Dewey Decimal System and were introduced to the magic of call waiting and caller ID. In junior high school, they used AOL dial-up internet and participated in online chat rooms. In high school, they got their first email address outside of AOL and got pagers and eventually cell phones with texting capabilities. A few years later, they got the first iteration of what are now the ever-present iPhones and iPads. Everything became "smart," during their formative years, from phones to thermostats to doorbells and more. They're now incorporating artificial intelligence and augmented reality into their daily lives.

Gen Xers and Boomers experienced these changes, too. *But we didn't have to deal with them during the years when our personalities and proclivities were still being shaped.*

It's one thing to process change as an adult. It's a whole different deal to be a preteen and feel like the world is shifting so much around you that you can't find your footing. It's no wonder some of these Millennials seem scattered, uncertain, or even cynical (we'll touch on this some more later). It's like we threw out the entire playbook that worked during their most critical years of growth, and then gave them a whole new playbook—before they had the tools to adjust and pivot.

At the same time, helicopter parents tried to prepare Millennials for success by signing them up for football, hockey, lacrosse, clarinet, piano, drama, private Pig Latin lessons, Ukrainian egg decorating, and other extracurriculars they thought would position them to get accepted into the best college possible. That, the parents believed, would then earn them the best job out of school. It was a noble goal, of course.

Unfortunately, this approach left many Millennials completely unprepared for the demands of the workplace, without Mom and Dad there to help.

All hope isn't lost, though. Just like small changes to our diets and exercise programs can reverse weight gain and poor health, small changes to how we interact with Millennials in the workplace can reverse the negative consequences of decades of helicopter parenting and misunderstandings.

I, too, have experienced the exasperation of trying to lead Millennials the **wrong** way in the past. And we can all learn from and avoid the trial and error I experienced as I went from frustrated with them to now valuing my Millennial employees as an integral part of my success.

The reality is when we invest in Millennials and use the strategies in this book, we can get exponential positive returns.

I've watched my own department here at 22squared go from an "investment" to a "profit center." A workplace that uses the skills, imagination, and connectivity of Millennials will experience benefits like:

- Rising profits
- Increased productivity
- Trendspotting
- Arriving first to market
- Outlasting the competition

But far more important than the bullet-pointed, hard-lined results are workplaces that harness the power of Millennials, where people actually *enjoy* spending their days. Employees feel valued and connected. They feel understood and included. *This is why they produce more.* It's human nature to want to perform well for the people you care most about.

THE FLIP SIDE: WHAT IF NOTHING CHANGES?

Let's say our generation just keeps on doing things the way we've always done them—rolling our eyes at these "entitled brats" and gritting our teeth anytime one of them chimes in during a meeting. Our companies will soon be overrun with people who hate working there. They'll do the bare minimum to keep their paychecks, because who enjoys helping those who treat them poorly prosper? The first time our employees see a chance to jump ship, they will. We'll spend vast amounts of time and money rehiring and retraining . . . more Millennials.

(Let's remember that Millennials are 35% of the workforce and will be 75% by 2030.)

We'll exhaust our resources on things that don't matter to the people we're looking to motivate. We'll waste money on benefits they don't care about, training that doesn't work with them, and recruiting efforts that aren't designed to let the best candidates rise to the top.

We'll try to hold on to the old ways.

We'll shut our eyes to the opportunity standing right in front of us.

Companies will fold. Many may even have to declare bankruptcy. After all, if leaders at the company can't work with 75% of the labor force, the future probably isn't very bright for them.

The cycle will repeat unless we decide to become solopreneurs (and good luck making *that* work).

The future would be bleak.

And if we can't get this Millennial generation right, just wait until we meet the ones behind them. Generation Z will eat us alive *unless we're willing to shift how we do business to better recruit, motivate, and lead Millennials to capitalize on our Millennial workforce.*

Millennials are shaking up the business world, and they have incredible adaptability. When we learn to bring out their best, they will catapult our companies to the top of our industries. Look at Airbnb, Lyft, Facebook, Pinterest, and Groupon—all founded by Millennials—and see how channeling Millennial energy can deliver tremendous success.

The *great* news?

Getting the most out of Millennials doesn't require more money— nor does it require having Ping Pong tables and beer kegs in the breakroom.

All it takes is a small shift in where we direct our resources. This book contains cost-effective, quick strategies we can implement to ensure that the Millennial workforce becomes a key driver to success.

Ansley and Angela: A Tale of Two Views

Ansley Williams is a Millennial who's been working at 22squared for three and a half years. Before landing at 22squared, Ansley bounced around companies, struggling to find herself and real worth. She found herself misunderstood and micromanaged at other companies. You'll hear more about her story later, but she began to thrive as we immediately implemented many of the concepts in this book. She won the respect of key clients and is now managing a team of her own.

Ansley's story highlights an important point about Millennials in the workforce. Sometimes—many times—we have the right people in front of us but just aren't getting their best work out of them. While that's sometimes a *them* issue, it's often an *us* issue.

Take a friend of mine whom I'll call Angela to protect her privacy. Recently, she came to me seeking advice because she couldn't keep her workforce motivated. Angela was an operations person who worked at a large digital analytics firm overseeing a department of 20, and she was not a visionary.

She plopped on a couch in my house, petting Tilly as I asked her if she saw herself as inspiring, and she quickly said no. I then asked how old her workforce was and she replied, "They're all Millennials."

"Those Millennials—they're killing baby kittens!" I joked, but then focused on the situation at hand. She went on to talk about her high turnover rate and their lack of drive and enthusiasm for the work.

Angela needed two things: first, a ying to her yang. Millennials crave well-rounded leadership—a combination of inspiring and organizational. If we're only one of those (like Angela was) we need to find someone else to fill in the gaps and serve as guide and coach.

Second, she needed to introduce some chaos and inspiration to the order she brought to the group. She was treating all Millennials the same, the older ones and the younger ones. But with everything that happened in the world between 1981 and 1996, older and younger Millennials had substantially different experiences and developed similarly different needs and tendencies.

"Millennials are unmanageable," Angela said. She thought if the Millennials in my agency were producing, I must have a room full of Ping Pong tables and beer kegs. And I must have a drawer full of participation trophies to hand out on a daily basis. She'd already gone through the trouble of putting a nitro coffee tap in place and even a "cereal bar" where people could pour themselves a bowl of their choice, but nothing seemed to impact the morale or culture.

The truth is my ad agency does keep beer around, but it's not why you might think. We host events in our office from time to time. Because one of our amazing clients is SweetWater Brewery, we make sure to keep plenty of their beers on hand. We also do have a Ping Pong table or two around, although they tend to function as conference or coworking tables. I can't remember the last time a Ping Pong game broke out.

And we do award prizes to employees, but *definitely* not just for showing up. They are *not* participation trophies. They're awards. We reward things we want to get more of—productivity, going above and beyond, and supporting coworkers. We love awarding prizes to employees who best exemplify those traits and show tangible ways they've helped *change* the organization or help a client.

Yet everything we see about Millennials labels them as terrible workers.

Holding on to a belief that Millennials are out to take all they can get from our company—without giving anything in return—can understandably make us avoid hiring them.

But Millennials are far from entitled, lazy, or ruining anything. In my experience, and that of other business leaders I'll share, they can be humble, hardworking, and the best thing to happen to your business—if you lead them well. As for "screwed," they may be, especially if we as leaders continue to insist on running our businesses as if it were the 1970s.

They're also a tricky generation to lead because they themselves are so diverse. As my episode with Angela illustrates, we must recognize the nuances between the older Millennials and the younger Millennials.

FIRST PERSON PROBLEMS

It's hard writing this book in the first person. I've been trained and conditioned that we all excel as a team and should avoid at all costs taking all the credit for something. So which is better—we or I? If we're working with Millennials early in their career, we must encourage them to use I to assert themselves. As they progress, their I becomes We. It's infuriating for Millennials when a leader stands in front of a group and take credit for all their hard work (using I). Millennials must also understand the importance of augmenting our weaknesses with others' strengths.

When it comes to I, I also know that operations and order are not my strong suits—I like to build the big vision of where we're going, not necessarily the steps involved with how to make that a reality.

So, one of the critical pieces to my own success was finding that order. For example, the Social Media Department didn't really thrive (or make any money) until we brought on Genna Franconi to help bring the order and operations to complement my own chaos. She immediately agreed with my vision, but the group lacked any order from our pricing structure to our development tracks, promotional guidelines, and proper job titles with job descriptions—yeah, it was a bit of a mess in hindsight. But within a year of her arriving, the department was firing on all cylinders and had the largest growth offering of the agency. Builders need maintainers, and maintainers need builders (I must say that Genna is actually a mix of both). I had finally succeeded in hiring someone that could take my job from me (isn't that what they tell you?).

Recognizing the Changing Seasons of Life

Before digging deeper into the differences between older and younger Millennials, it's important for us to acknowledge one truth. Many subtleties of the differences we feel between us and the Millennials have more to do with the relevant seasons of life than some diabolical plan to avoid work or work only remotely. Only a few years out of school, they are still learning. That's why we can teach them attitude and ethic expectations instead of formally assessing those attributes while they are still a work in progress.

Millennials as a group are in their twenties and thirties as of the writing of this book. That means the younger ones are dating, getting married, and beginning to have kids. As they get older, they're having second or third kids, scouting school districts, and laying down roots. The whole time, they're feeling their way around the corporate world trying to discover what they love to do and are good at doing. Earlier you heard from Tommy Breedlove, a friend of mine who helps emerging leaders build a fulfilling personal and professional life without giving up the ability to build wealth. He says that Millennials are squarely in the midst of searching for their Area of Brilliance in the world. This is where your passions, talents, and profits intersect. You and I may have found ours. But most Millennials haven't, especially the younger ones.

Even the older Millennials have kids who are not grown and out of the house. Many don't have disposable income to splurge on two long vacations per year, so they need to take more mini-vacations to decompress from the stresses of a demanding corporate environment. And they don't have decades of experience finding their Area of Brilliance.

That raises the question of whether the behaviors or tendencies those of us from an older generation see as disinterest or lack of dedication is actually a natural and reasonable byproduct of the season of life both older and younger Millennials find themselves in. We need to consider that question as we dig deeper into the differences between older and younger Millennials as well as when we evaluate the Millennials who work on our teams.

In other words, are they *really* lazy, or do they just have two toddlers keeping them up all night? Are they *really* not interested in doing what it takes to make partner, or do they have three preteens who need help with homework and shuttles to soccer practice? Do they *really* not care about the big sales pitch, or are they dealing with the time commitment and stress of planning weddings and putting together seating charts that keep their soon-to-be in-laws far enough away from their crazy uncle who always knows the wrong thing to say?

Here are more details that may explain many of the differences between Millennials and older generations plus the many differences that exist between the older and younger Millennials.

The Older Millennials

Older Millennials spent their early childhood in much the same way as Xers. But when they hit adolescence and puberty—their hormones shifting—everything around them started shifting, too. "You've got mail!" AOL opened up a whole new world: the world-wide web. Huge and cumbersome cell phones became staples in cars "just in case" there was an emergency. These Millennials didn't have mobile phones until they were getting ready to graduate college in the early 2000s.

Older Millennials didn't grow up in the technological age. They started out making mix tapes and recording their favorite shows on VHS. They then shifted to listening to music on tiny MP3 players—all in less than a decade.

In addition to the technological advances, these older Millennials faced what felt to them like a total bait and switch of everything their parents sold them as the right way to succeed. I'm talking about the Great Recession of the late 2000s.

Like Boomers and Xers, these older Millennials started out playing by the rules. They went to school, studied hard, got degrees. Some even went to grad school. They did everything their parents told them to do to get a good, stable job. They even took entry-level jobs in fields where they thought they could grow. They put in long hours and showed up ready to work.

And then the rug got pulled out from under them.

The Great Recession hit, leaving these older Millennials—the ones who had done everything Boomers and Xers told them they were "supposed" to do—high and dry.

They were "downsized," "right-sized," or "released."

As a result, this group of Millennials developed a level of cynicism not seen in prior generations of workers. And that makes sense. The Xers and Boomers who "played by the rules" generally got their steady paycheck and annual promotions.

Yes, *some* of the older generations lost jobs in the recession, too, but only after a decade or more of steady employment. The older Millennials lost their jobs just as their student loans became due.

Older Millennials became enamored with Mark Zuckerberg and other start-up disruptors who have careers much different from their parents' 9-to-5, loyalty-driven jobs.

The Younger Millennials

Younger Millennials didn't experience change in the same way as their older counterparts. They *grew up with* cell phones and iPods. By the time they were hitting adolescence, smartphones were a staple.

These Millennials never had to go to the library to do research for a term paper. They had the internet at their fingertips. They never had to sit home by the phone hoping their crush would call. They went on with their plans knowing that a text message could come in at any time.

This level of instantaneous answers and connectivity almost redefined their sense of time. Two minutes of TV commercials seems like an eternity to them. A five-minute wait seems like hours to them. It might seem crazy to older generations, but it's what they grew up on (mind you, they're also binge-watching Netflix series for hours on end). This expectation for instantaneous connection spilled into their work life, too. When they entered the workforce, they were handed Blackberries or had emails added to their phone. They were expected to be available and respond to emails right away. Everything about their work and home life became real time.

It's natural, then, that this bled into their desire for connectivity and feedback from their leaders. It might seem needy to us, but when put in the context of how they grew up and what's expected of them, it makes sense. And they don't *mean* it as being needy. Their internal clocks are faster than ours. When we give them connection and feedback in a way that fits within that structure—both positive *and negative* feedback—we can keep them motivated and working hard. More on that later.

They also weren't forced out of the job market when the recession hit. Most of them were still in high school, so they had time to adjust to the new rules of the working world. But while they didn't *experience* the lack of loyalty in corporate America, they did observe it. They saw their parents laid off from jobs they had worked for decades. They felt the effects firsthand as their families' retirement savings disappeared, leaving nothing for their college funds or their parents' future.

That opened their eyes to the idea that they needed to get scrappy and innovate to survive. Security became less about working their way up a company for 30 years and waiting for the gold watch and more about building security independent of the company. That way, they didn't *need* that job to have a secure future.

In other words, we showed them they can't depend on us to protect and provide for themselves, and we inadvertently inspired them to forge their own paths in the workplace.

But now we complain that these Millennials "don't respect authority" and are "too easily distracted." When we look into what really happened and what they experienced their whole life, it's easy to see how they might hesitate to trust us as leaders. Everyone is now talking about the Generation Z that is following the Millennials, and in reality, they are very much the same as these younger Millennials in their attitudes and needs, only taken to a whole other level of intensity. So don't fret—see this book as the Generation Z Whisperer as well as one that will help you out with the Millennials. You can apply this same analysis and these same strategies to help you avoid getting eaten alive by Generation Z as they begin to enter the workforce in numbers.

ACCEPTING HOW WE GOT HERE

There's no denying that we—you, I, and the rest of the Xers and Boomers—have actually helped to create the very dynamics we complain about within the Millennial workforce. It's not a good thing or a bad thing. It's just the reality.

We created—and handed to them—much of the technology that "distracts" them. Again, it's not a good thing or a bad thing. And it's not going anywhere.

We ruthlessly terminated both them and their parents during the Great Recession. We modeled for them that loyalty is nonexistent in the corporate world. We may have needed to do so to save our companies from collapsing, but—like many of us say about the Millennials—it's not logical to expect there to be no consequences to having done so. We laid a bunch of people off, and now we're trusted less.

We made buying a house scary. *We* made ordering groceries online easy. *We* helicopter-parented them. *We* told them *not* to get jobs during high school because they needed to fill their plates with extracurricular and philanthropic pursuits that the best colleges would find attractive. These harsh-but-true realizations must be conceded if we want to move forward. We set ourselves up for the very scenarios that now frustrate us.

But as awful as that sounds, it's actually *great news*! **Because if we are the ones who knocked the equilibrium off kilter, we are the ones who can restore it—with some simple and practical strategies.** The first step is understanding that most of what we've thought about Millennials is wrong. The vast majority of them are not lazy, entitled, *or* screwed. They are the future of our businesses. They are the innovators and the implementers.

And we get to harness the power of Millennials in our workforce. It's not just the size of the generation that's important for the future of business, either. We've raised Millennials to value different things. We've raised them to not need or want things our generation traditionally needed or wanted—Harley Davidsons, massive McMansions (tiny house, anyone?). We've also raised them to care about things we didn't focus too much time on when we were their age, such as a rafting trip on the Colorado River instead of a shiny new Schwinn. We created the eco-minded culture that may see plastic bags and plastic straws disappear.

This is true all over the world. Business leaders assume that Millennials are less loyal than Boomers and Generation Xers. But a multigenerational study of 1784 employees across 12 countries and six industries compiled by the IBM Institute for Business Value's 2014 Executive Report reveals that while 47% of Gen Xers would leave their company for more money or a more innovative environment, only 42% of Millennials would do so.

Millennials have a reputation of bucking the system and questioning authority. But in reality, 70% of Baby Boomers think their organization is inept at addressing customer concerns, while this number is only 60% among Millennials.[6]

It's up to us. It's our choice as to whether we do the work and implement strategies to better understand Millennials and learn to attract, retain, and motivate them. If we do, our future is bright. We can become more profitable. We can attract the best employees and get them to do their best work. And we can *finally* achieve the flexibility to not need our fingerprints on everything in the office to make sure it's done how we want it. We will have the best employees from the biggest generational pool of workers focused, motivated, and working together.

But if we ignore this rising demographic or write off the realities of how we raised them and what motivates them to perform, we do so at our own peril.

When we harness the positivity and ingenuity of Millennials, we create a loyal workforce that will go above and beyond to serve our companies well.

Millennials care about authenticity and purpose, and they want to feel like they're contributing to a goal beyond just paying their bills. They see and crave the potential businesses have to improve the world around them. Three-quarters of respondents in the 2018 Deloitte Millennial Survey report they see business as having an opportunity to help solve society's economic, environmental, and social challenges, with a particular focus on improving our climate and minimize the misuse of natural resources.[7]

We'll discuss how we can capitalize on Millennials' desire to be a force for good in the world and simultaneously increase their positive impact within our organizations.

And we'll go far beyond Google autocomplete and anecdotes for support. We'll draw heavily from the latest and most comprehensive research about Millennials, how they work, what motivates them, and more. We'll share many stories and examples to emphasize the points go far beyond the anecdotes.

The bottom line is that some of us (lots of us) have misunderstood and mismanaged Millennials. I've been as guilty as anyone at times. I've experienced the power of leading a team of Millennials. I, too, have misunderstood and mismanaged them at times. But I've also experienced the incredible power a motivated Millennial team brings to business.

What Millennials Really Want, and Why it's Easy and Critical for Us to Give it to Them

Millennials are eager to give their best for purpose-driven companies. The organizations that have tapped into this fact are catapulting past their counterparts who've stayed mired in the old ways.

When we focus on *inspiring* Millennials, creating a *culture of transparency*, and giving Millennials *autonomy within structure*, we'll succeed in the modern workplace. I'll say it once, and I'll say it again, and again, and—well, you get the point.

As *The Economist* reports, a poll of 5,000 workers found that 41% of Millennials agreed that "employees should do what their manager tells them, even when they can't see the reason for it"—compared with 30% of Boomers and 30% of Gen Xers.

But what if we aren't willing to shift our view of Millennials and take these three actions to help them succeed? We will go the way of Kodak, Blockbuster, and Sears . . . outpaced by those who were willing to be adaptable.

How Millennials Drive Profit with Purpose

What does it take to go from zero to billion-dollar valuation within eight years? Purpose. Millennials will work hard to make us profitable *if* they first know the purpose behind our work. This generation is incredibly focused on leaving a mark on society. They'll give us much more when they believe we're not only looking out for our bottom line.

Take Warby Parker, for example. The revolutionary eyewear company was founded by four MBA students determined to do good in the world *and* make a profit. Since 2010, Warby Parker has not only made a dramatic impact in the marketplace (achieving a $1.75 billion valuation within eight years) but has also distributed more than a million pairs of eyeglasses to people in developing countries.

Amidst predictions of the death of brick-and-mortar retailers, Warby Parker, now 1,400 employees strong, laid out plans to open 100 physical storefronts.

Then there's Patagonia, whose mission statement reads:

> For us at Patagonia, a love of wild and beautiful places demands participation in the fight to save them, and to help reverse the steep decline in the overall environmental health of our planet. We donate our time, services, and at least 1% of our sales to hundreds of grassroots environmental groups all over the world who work to help reverse the tide.
>
> We know that our business activity—from lighting stores to dyeing shirts—creates pollution as a byproduct. So we work steadily to reduce those harms. We use recycled polyester in many of our clothes and only organic, rather than pesticide-intensive, cotton.
>
> Staying true to our core values during thirty-plus years in business has helped us create a company we're proud to run and work for. And our focus on making the best products possible has brought us success in the marketplace.[8]

Or how about American Standard's "Flush For Good" campaign, which 22squared created with American Standard. For each American Standard Champion toilet sold in 2013, a life-saving latrine pan was donated to people in developing communities. The campaign resulted in over 500,000 donated toilet pans. This is exactly the type of promotion that attracts big-hearted, service-based Millennial workers. These are the Millennials we want on our teams. They'll come in early, stay late, and work weekends when they believe they're part of a team that's doing great work in the world. Most of the team members who worked on this campaign were Millennials and had no problem putting in the long hours to get it to market because they knew they were doing good in the world.

Millennials desire to work for these types of organizations that espouse goals and incentives beyond making more money. This generation wants to know that the organizations they work for are serious about making a positive impact in the world.

These are just a few examples of how building a purpose-driven culture can lead to higher revenue and profits. We'll talk about more examples when we talk about motivating Millennials and how to get the best work from your Millennial team members. But there's no denying the impact of purpose on profits with a Millennial workforce.

In one Deloitte Millennial Survey, 86% of respondents agreed with the statement that the "success of a business should be measured in terms of more than just its financial performance."[9] Meanwhile, 65% of Millennials in the study believed that their companies' activities benefit society in some way. Environmental challenges (24%) topped the list of challenges that demand the attention of business, followed by inequality (23%), skill and resource shortage (16%), societal challenges (15%), external environment (10%), financial challenges (8%) and innovation (7.5%).[10] Because Millennials make up more than a third of the workforce—and will constitute 75% of workers by 2030—this focus on meaningful work must be taken seriously.

The more our companies can be purpose-driven with authenticity, the more we will attract, engage, and retain Millennials. Purpose creates positivity and energy in the workplace, while a focus on profits creates negativity and fatigue. It's time to stop chasing the dollar bills and start chasing the real-world skills that will bring about change for good. For Millennials, purpose is paramount. By combining these three elements, we will get the highest and best work out of our Millennial employees:

A. Purpose
B. Profit {but this rarely means pure financial profit; Millennials crave social capital}
C. Acknowledgement

As shown in the earlier examples, Millennials long to be a part of a culture that gives back. They want to be part of a movement that extends beyond themselves and leaves a legacy. Our messages need to be about the *purpose* behind our work, even more than about the profits we want to make.

We must inspire Millennials to get the most out of them. This is imperative, and there's really no getting around it. A visionary must be at the helm of any Millennial workforce—and this applies to the company's substructure, too.

A company-wide purpose is not enough to keep Millennials on track if their department leader lacks vision. So how do we work around this if we don't consider ourselves to be inspirational or visionary? We bring in reinforcements. Every department and division needs someone who reassures Millennials that their efforts extend beyond the company's bottom line. If we don't currently have those leaders in place in our organizations, we must hire co-leaders who exhibit these visionary traits.

We don't always have to hire from the outside. We can often take a look at our current workforce and simply reshuffle some employees to ensure that each subset has an inspirational leader at the top of the organizational chart. Order needs some chaos, and chaos needs some order—that's why an inspirational leader can be matched with an operational leader and vice versa. We spend so much time trying to train our leaders to be Swiss Army knives whereas in fact they are sharpest when they are visionaries *or* integrators—not both.

Deloitte's research proves this: 44% of Millennials believe in the ability of business leaders to make a positive impact—more than religious leaders (33%) or political leaders (19%). When we can tie purpose with profit and acknowledgement, we'll get unimagined results from our Millennial workforce. Remember that "profit" to Millennials doesn't mean just cash. I've written a whole chapter on how you can reward and recognize your team to get their best work. Feel free to jump ahead for ideas on how you can incentivize your Millennial workforce.

A Culture of Transparency

Millennials *hate* hypocrisy. As a leader, we must do the things we say we'll do and play fair across the board. Building transparency into our companies will ensure that we attract and retain quality Millennial employees. One way that Millennial-friendly companies are using this to their advantage is with financial transparency.

Note that the word "transparency" doesn't mean complete and total access. For example, Ben Kirshner, Founder and CEO of the award-winning digital marketing agency, Elite SEM, espouses a form of "open book management" within his company. (Fortune Magazine has called Elite SEM "the best workplace for Millennials.")

Elite SEM employees have access to company financials through monthly metrics meetings and quarterly financial deep dives. Kirshner has implemented a policy of salary transparency, too, but note that this doesn't mean that every employee knows what his or her office mate earns. Instead, Kirshner breaks down salaries by business team. This lets the more entry-level workers know that the C-suite officers aren't taking an exorbitant share of the financial pie.

There's a great benefit to this type of financial transparency. When times get lean, everyone is inspired to work harder and get more creative. The entire team knows what's necessary for pay raises and bonuses to take effect. For Elite SEM, when it came time to vote on whether the company would take private equity, Millennials got on board because they could clearly understand the financial stakes. There's no downside to giving this sort of access, either. Millennials are accustomed to seeing the behind-the-scenes info on pretty much everyone in their lives . . . from their best friends to their favorite pop stars and actors. *In showing financials openly, we're speaking to them in a language they understand*. They'll reward our communication with consistent efforts to meet our expectations.

In another example of transparency, Ben stages town-hall-style meetings, tackling some of the employees' toughest questions including, on a recent occasion, "What do you do all day?" This gave him the opportunity to communicate how much stuff he does that no one else wants to do.

Autonomy Within Structure

A good friend of mine often says, "Build them a hallway, not railroad tracks." Millennials exhibit a high level of responsibility when they are given the freedom to creatively discover solutions for issues the company may be facing. They thrive under a "loose structure."

Millennial employees can take ownership in their own work. When they have a personal stake in their work, they take pride in its quality.

Remember that our Millennial employees are our greatest asset in navigating the fickle hype cycle of today's business culture. Trends come and go in the blink of an eye (or the click of a cursor).

Do you remember the days before swimming pools were filled with swan floats? That trend started when pop star Taylor Swift broadcast her love for the pool toy—and then-boyfriend Calvin Harris—via Instagram.

Millennials latched on quickly, and the swan float has been a ubiquitous summertime accessory ever since. Fidget spinners and Snuggies, meanwhile? *Buh-bye.*

We can give Millennials free rein enough to let them help our company shine while other organizations shuffle along in circa 2006-Uggs. Millennials, with incredible tech-savviness, have the desire to change organizations in a world they are disrupting on a daily basis.

QUICK SUMMARY

- Millennials are a company's greatest asset. They are the largest segment of the workforce today, so it's worth the time to learn how to leverage their skills.
- The importance of the Millennial generation is only growing. Millennials will comprise 75% of our workforce and customers by 2030. If our relationship with them is poor, the future of our companies will be bleak.
- There are a lot of negative stereotypes about Millennials. These stereotypes are hurting businesses way more than they're hurting Millennials. These stereotypes are also wrong.
- Statistics show Millennials are actually hardworking yet we continue to malign them with biases and misconceptions.
- Yet, our biases and misconceptions keep us from maximizing the full potential of our Millennial workforce.
- Both older and younger Millennials were shaped by the environment they grew up in. (The same is true for every generation.) The fact is, we created them. We created this environment. It's not wrong or right. It's just reality. We can complain, or we can learn what makes them tick, get the best ones working for us, and put them in a position to do their best work.
- There are three things we *must* do as leaders to take full advantage of our Millennial staff. These three steps are only the foundation for making the most of your Millennial talent.

» Inspire the Millennial workforce. Millennials are inspired if they know that the organization they work for is serious about making a positive impact in the world.

» Create a culture of transparency. Millennials crave transparency. That's not to say we give every Millennial every piece of information about ourselves or our companies. But we can get more from our workforce when they understand more about what drives profits and how our profits impact the greater purpose of our companies.

» Give Millennials autonomy *within* structure. Millennials need direction, but they also need autonomy. To paraphrase a good friend of mine, we need to build them hallways, not railroad tracks. Hallways guide them where we need them to go but give them *some* freedom and flexibility within that structure.

MAKE IT HAPPEN.

We're going to end each chapter—and the book—with strategies to help put the information, stories, and strategies to work for you and your organization. If you're in senior management, go through the Make it Happen sections from a bigger-picture perspective. Consider them within the context of your entire organization and the teams and team leaders who report to you.

If you're a team leader managing a smaller team within an organization, go through them briefly on an organizational level, but focus more energy on your team's role in the greater company and the role of each of your team members.

I'll share a few example answers throughout the book to get some ideas flowing. You can download a PDF with all of these exercises, plus more sample answers from me at the Resources page, TheMillennialWhisperer. com/BookResources.

This Make it Happen section focuses on the three things we must do as leaders to take full advantage of our Millennial staff, inspire, build transparency, and provide autonomy within structure.

Inspiration

- What positive impact does your company make in the world? How do your products or services make a positive impact? This doesn't need to be some *huge* impact. You don't need to be curing cancer. Even small but meaningful impacts in your clients' or customers' lives can help inspire your Millennial workforce.
  - » For example, 22squared helps connect our clients' products and services with customers who need them. We do that through our ad services, but we do our best work when we find the best fits for our customers, promoting their products or services to people who need and want them.
- How does the team contribute to the organization's impact?
  - » How does each team member contribute to the impact?
  - » What small wins or hurdles can you set up to acknowledge your team and each team member is staying on track?
  - » Challenge your team to each write down three things in their notebook or on a Post-It note of small things they'll do to have some sort of step toward that impact. Keep it to only three things at a time; with each win, a new one goes up. Soon enough, the collective impact can be palpable and

each small win attributed (and celebrated) to the person who gets it done.

Transparency

- What information can you share with your team about:
- The role profits play into the bigger purpose of the company
- How their role impacts profits
- Why that's important to their role
- How you're personally evaluated in your job performance

Autonomy Within Structure

- What are the main goals of the organization?
- What are the main goals of each (or your) team or department?
  - » One year from now, what do you need to have accomplished at the company and team or department level to consider it a success?
  - » What boundaries can you set up to keep people moving in the right direction to achieve that one goal without having to micromanage each step of the way?
  - » Now that you've gone through these core foundational questions, it's time to create a culture where Millennials will thrive.

CHAPTER 1

CREATING A CULTURE FOR MILLENNIALS TO THRIVE

Attracting, Retaining, and Setting up Millennials for Success

We all hate to go to the dentist—unless, perhaps, we go to the Atlanta Dental Spa (ADS), where Dr. Peter Boulden, DMD, has combined luxurious pampering with the traditional poking and prodding, plus a healthy dose of purpose. More than 80% of Dr. Boulden's employees are Millennials, and he's developed specific strategies to help them feel they are making an impact so that they'll give their top effort to the practice.

At the beginning of each month, Dr. Boulden sends around a survey with a list of charitable organizations that ADS is considering supporting. The team then votes on which organization will receive that month's ADS Cares dollars.

There's a catch, however. ADS must hit certain numbers before cutting the check at the end of the month. Remember how we discussed the importance of transparency? Each of Dr. Boulden's offices has a morning meeting where they discuss how close they are to reaching the goals necessary to give away the ADS Cares dollars that month. This empowers ADS Millennial employees to work hard toward hitting the financial benchmark necessary for donating the funds.

Since ADS's implementation of this democratic charity-choosing strategy, there's only been *one month* when the practice didn't hit its financial goals and wasn't able to give away funds to the chosen charity.

Dr. Boulden says he hears much more from his employees about their excitement in giving away funds to philanthropic organizations than he does about them receiving their own personal financial bonuses.

He has created a triple win by including his Millennial employees in the decision about where the company's money goes.

1. *The company wins.* Transparency and fairness have allowed all of his employees to understand that they must remain profitable in order to give the way they all desire to give.

2. *The owners win.* With the entire team pushing hard to meet financial targets so that they can financially bless their philanthropic organizations of choice, Dr. Boulden sees continued healthy revenues and profits in his practice.

3. *The employees win.* Dr. Boulden's team feels heard as they get to choose where the charitable dollars go. They're seeing the efforts of their work pay off very concretely in the difference they making within the community.

This triple win serves two purposes for ADS, Dr. Boulden, and the Millennial employees. First, it gives everyone an opportunity to get involved in philanthropic causes greater than themselves. Second, it creates *alignment* between company, employer, and employees, positioning them as working together to crave and strive toward a common, mutually beneficial goal.

In addition, by showing his employees the numbers, it reinforces the importance of healthy business finances. His employees recognize that it would be irresponsible to donate toward a cause if the business wasn't healthy financially, and the best way to be able to make more positive contributions to the world is to work hard and give back from a position of financial strength.

ADS Cares is just one example of how creating the right culture for Millennials, with simple tweaks to the infrastructure already in place, can pay off in big ways.

THE MESSAGE IS CLEAR

Remember those 10,000-plus Millennials surveyed by Deloitte in 2018? They emphasize that a company's culture is paramount to their loyalty.

"The message is clear," write the study authors. "Young workers are eager for business leaders to be proactive about making a positive impact in society—and to be responsive to employees' needs." The top five attributes that make an organization an attractive employer to Millennials, in order of importance, are:

1. Financial rewards/benefits (63% of respondents)
2. Positive workplace culture (52%)
3. Flexibility (50%)
4. Opportunities for continuous learning (48%)
5. Well-being programs and incentives (33%)

"Respondents are disappointed that business leaders' priorities don't seem to align with their own," conclude the authors, "but where matches exist, the perception is that those companies are more successful, have more stimulating work environments, and do a better job of developing talent."

Rise and Shine

Once we decide to get serious about making the most of our Millennial employees, we must ensure that our company culture makes them feel like a part of the team. We need systems and procedures in place that will allow Millennials to succeed when they join our organizations.

If we don't give our Millennials workers the opportunity to succeed—and on their terms—they'll leave. Millennials do not have the same concept of loyalty as Generation Xers and Boomers. They *can* have incredible staying power, but only after we've proven that we have their best interests at heart as much as we do our own bottom line.

Research backs this up. The Deloitte Millennial Survey 2018 found that 43% of Millennials envision leaving their jobs within two years, a number that grows higher among those working for companies that prioritize profit. The survey also revealed that 52% of Millennials believe that a "positive workplace culture" is very important, a close second to financial rewards (63%).[11]

We don't want to get stuck having to recruit and train new people who will only be as committed to us as we are to them. Let's keep the Millennials we *do* recruit feeling engaged so that we can save the time, money, and energy we'd spend on rehiring. We must create a culture that enhances Millennials' sense of security and appreciation within our company.

If we don't, we'll watch them walk out the door.

The best way to craft a company culture that welcomes Millennials is to allow them to craft it with us.

At 22squared, for example, my Millennial team decided to create an Instagram handle of #22culture, proudly displaying it in our lobby. Now, more than 3,800 photos fill the feed, documenting everything from

Frosted Flakes and Field Day to Irish dancing and internships. It's good, clean fun that automatically invests Millennials in our success. When we implement a company culture that allows Millennials to thrive— engineering an environment of mutual respect and admiration—we get the bonus side effect of weeding out the kind of Millennials we don't want in our companies.

WHEN MILLENNIALS WORK BEST

Millennials work best when they have a say in the work. It's important to remember the three things Millennials need:

A. Purpose
B. Profit {but not necessarily the traditional kind of profit}
C. Acknowledgement

Let's focus on the last one for a minute: *acknowledgement.*

Millennials deeply desire to be seen. Their behavior on social media shows just a small sliver of their need for attention and affirmation. This generation has grown up judging themselves by the number of "friends" on Facebook or "likes" on Instagram they accumulate. (Many younger Millennials actually have multiple Instagram accounts for different friend groups and purposes.) When we make Millennials part of crafting our company culture, they'll feel included and valued. And when Millennials feel included and valued, they'll give us their very best.

Two effective tools to incorporate a sense of acknowledgement into the workplace are team-bonding activities and incorporating humor into the workplace.

If you're just starting out, team dinners and other team-building outings can be a good way to make our Millennial team members feel acknowledged. Just including them in activities that are not directly work-related helps make them feel noticed and important.

While these experiences are a great start, there is a more effective formula for building powerful team relationships. Based on extensive psychological research made popular by the No.1 highest viewed TED talk and the books Daring Greatly and The Power of Vulnerability, researcher Brené Brown has shown that vulnerability—the willingness to be "all in" even when you know it can mean failing and hurting—is the most powerful ingredient for deep human connection. So I've found that the most effective kinds of team experiences are ones that challenge us to get outside our comfort zone, face difficult and uncomfortable circumstances, and overcome it together as a team embracing vulnerability, courage, and adaptability.

An Atlanta-based start-up, Vestigo, helps companies create these kinds of experiences through powerful adventure-based team initiatives using every kind of adventure sport imaginable from hiking to rappelling to jet suit flying (with Gravity.co). While these opportunities are particularly effective in increasing Millennial engagement, they can have powerful outcomes for employees of all ages. The team members most apprehensive toward the experience and least willing to get outside their comfort zone are often the ones who benefit the most from doing it.

To understand this concept in practice, let's observe the campaign Vestigo created for Bennett Thrasher, known as BT, a 300-person Atlanta-based accounting firm famous for its incredible culture and dedication to its core value of family. To emphasize that core value, Vestigo created a powerful initiative involving the entire company in an epic adventure and audacious goal of hiking the entire Georgia section of the Appalachian Trail (AT). The effort would raise funds and awareness for Down Syndrome as BT employee Brittany had just given birth to a daughter, Sutton, with the genetic disorder.

Together, the BT team members completed a collective total of 1,529.8 miles hiked for this "BT on the AT" challenge and raised over $7,055 for Gigi's Playhouse Down Syndrome Achievement Center. The company achieved even more than philanthropic success. First, there was the incredible publicity when a news reporter said he wanted to leave his station to work for BT. Second, the company experienced a 50% decrease in employee attrition. And finally, there were four drastic personal health breakthroughs from employees hiking, and likely many more that went untold. While these kinds of unconventional experiences take a large amount of courage and faith for a company to commit to, they are always worth the investment. As BT's founding chairman and partner said, "In 30 years of building Bennett Thrasher, this is the single greatest initiative we've ever done."

Another way to help Millennials feel included, validated, and acknowledged is by incorporating humor into the workplace. Being comfortable enough to be humorous with them creates an unspoken emotion of belonging, which can release stress and create stronger bonds among coworkers. In fact, researchers from Harvard Business School and Wharton School of Business have found that colleagues who make others laugh are seen as more confident, competitive, and higher in status—which is why one New York agency called Peppercomm regularly schools employees in stand-up comedy. At 22squared, we connected with Laughing Skull Lounge, an Atlanta comedy club, to train seven people from across the agency for five weeks. Called 22laughs, the program and final show were a major hit, and have motivated our Millennials even further.

Embracing Diversity and Inclusion

Meet Janis Middleton, a kick-ass Media Director at 22squared who has learned, and is working to evangelize, an important lesson about the most important aspect of company culture: diversity and inclusion.

Before coming to 22squared, Janis had worked at what she calls "a very, very diverse" agency in Atlanta. When she joined 22squared in 2013, she noticed that the culture was different from her previous agency, but in good ways. She touted learning more, being pushed to deliver great work, and most importantly, she felt that everyone was friendly and treated each other like family.

However, there were many moments where she didn't know her place. Not just in meetings, but simply being at 22squared. She felt very well-liked but didn't feel understood or sometimes heard.

"It was a bit of a shock," she now recalls, describing her mindset. "Do I speak up? How do I speak up?"

In 2016, Janis left for another agency for a role that would help to catapult her career. After she left, she noticed a shift in society, with social media at the forefront. At the time, the highly publicized police killings of two African-American men, Philando Castile and Alton Sterling, left many people of color at a standstill of what to do and found themselves unable to simply go to work and go about their day.

With Millennials growing up in the digital and social age, the news is always on for them. Whether good or bad, scrolling through the news feed can bring different types of content from advertising, family, and friends—or a gut-wrenching live video of Philando Castile taking his last breath.

This was a watershed moment for 22squared. It caused us to pause and listen to employees who could hardly put on a face and make it to work. Not only did 22squared listen, but the company also took action from the top down, starting with our CEO, Richard Ward.

22squared hired Al Vivian, a Diversity Expert and Founder and Owner of Basic Diversity Inc., to come in and conduct an assessment of what the agency was doing right and where they could improve. Vivian has worked with some of the largest brands, including several Fortune 100 companies.

Vivian conducted various focus groups with different genders, races, ethnicities, backgrounds, and titles. With the feedback from the focus groups, 22squared decided to create the Diversity and Inclusion Council to help the agency ensure all people are heard and felt, which is key to Millennials.

Because they are the most diverse generation, Millennials are hyperaware of diversity and inclusion challenges in society and in the workplace. Even if they don't fall under one of the minority groups, they have lived through one of the most divided times, and their circle of friends tend to be more diverse, so they possess empathy.

According to Anna Johansson, who wrote "The One Philosophical Difference That Sets Millennials Apart in Workplace Diversity," for *Forbes*, "more than half of Millennials would gladly take a pay cut to work for an employer who shares their values, and nearly half of Millennials (47%) actively look for diversity and inclusion programs in their prospective employers before finalizing a job decision."

Johansson also wrote: "This prioritization is practically motivated as much as it is ethically motivated. Today's Fortune 500 companies are overwhelmingly led by white males, yet companies that feature ethnic and racial diversity perform far better in almost every category; in fact, companies in the top quartile of diversity are 35% more likely to have above-average industry returns."

We've seen this play out with Janis and even outside of our organization. After ten months, Janis returned to 22squared because she felt that 22squared was indeed home. She felt that the opportunities and the people would aid her in creating a path to a future that aligned more with her goals and her purpose.

However, 22squared had noticeably changed. She felt as though she came back to a different culture. It was one that still had the amazing elements she loved before, but with a more diverse look and a more inclusive environment. It had become a place where she was "super proud" to be part of the team, a place where she felt included, and most importantly, supported. 22squared had landed on their purpose and put programs in place to help employees align with the agency purpose of "Together We Give Rise to Change," a societal purpose, as well as employee's individual purpose.

"Being able to come back and see it firsthand was a real shift," says Janis.

Diversity is one of the main issues and concerns on Millennial minds. According to one Glassdoor survey, two-thirds of candidates say that diversity is important to them when evaluating companies and job offers. So if you're not *proactively* doing something about diversity and inclusion—perhaps even hiring a chief diversity officer—you're already way behind.

Another example of the importance around diversity comes from a friend of mine who worked for years at a big tech firm. In the early years, she mentioned that this tech firm would only hire Ivy League school graduates. They soon realized their workers had very similar backgrounds and perspectives as one another; they needed differing perspectives.

They appeared diverse from the outside, but their diversity was limited; their workforce had all been filtered through the Ivy League educations. They began opening doors to people from all educational backgrounds and upbringings. The result was a big increase in innovation as well as new opinions and approaches that better matched their diverse customer set.

How to Let Millennials Rock the Boat (Without Capsizing the Ship)

Creating a Millennial culture is simpler than we think, and can touch us personally, too. Case in point: my 9-year working anniversary at 22squared. Yes, we celebrate *every* birthday and *every* working anniversary, with a buddy system that works beautifully. Every employee gets a reimbursable buddy budget but almost always adds his or her own money to it, plus a whole lot of creativity, to do something special for their assigned "buddy."

When I entered the office on my 9th working anniversary, a slew of colorful balloons was accompanied by a note that read, "In each of these balloons, you'll find some of our favorite moments, memories, and simply the things we admire about you. We feel so lucky to get to call you our fearless leader every day. Happy 9 Years." As I popped each balloon, a new note surfaced.

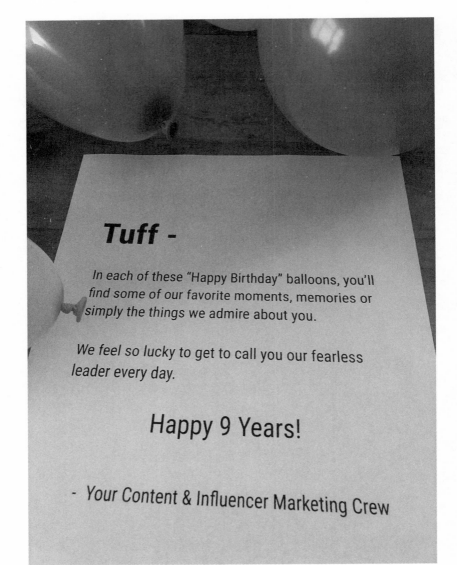

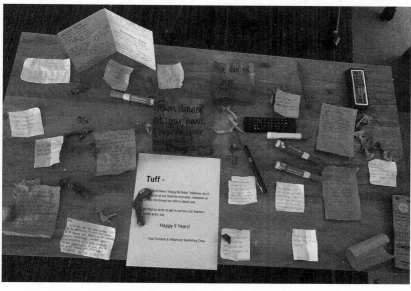

I was moved to tears—so proud of my team and their spirit of generosity, I headed to our President, Brandon Murphy, to share what had just happened. His remark? "You lead by example, Chris. We're showing appreciation to the Millennials we employ, and they're showing it back to us."

When we lead by example, our employees will honor us with their best and highest work.

Hero your people. Protect this house.

Millennials are incredibly concerned with *feelings*. They want and need to *sense* that they are appreciated. There is a myriad of ways in which we can convey our gratitude to our Millennial employees, but we must do so in a way that resonates at an emotional as well as an intellectual level. We can make them the *heroes* of our organizations.

Our employees *must* feel supported by leadership and that's why *every single* person on my team always knows that I'm willing to fall on a sword for him or her.

Ben Kirshner, the CEO of Elite SEM, puts the management and judgment power in the hands of his employees by taking a cue from Under Armour and telling his people to "protect this house!" This means protecting the amazing culture and holding high standards. Instead of putting pressure on management to hire the right candidates, Ben tends to push this power down to allow all employees to "protect this house." He lets his Millennial staff interview any potential new hires. They literally sit around a table and pepper their prospective colleague with questions. It's only natural, Ben postulates, that he permit his current employees to have a voice in choosing their new office mates. He's making his current employees heroes within his organization by giving them influence over who gets an offer of employment.

Ben prides himself on Elite SEM having greater than 90% employee retention and client retention rates. On Glassdoor.com (a ratings and reviews site for companies by employees), Ben has 100% approval rating and 4.8 stars out of 5 (impeccably high).

We can all lead our company's culture while still shaping policies in a way that gives Millennials a voice and allows them to feel *(yes, there's that feeling word again)* like they were the impetus of certain policies. We're not giving away complete control. We're being generous with our leadership and allowing Millennials to step up to the plate.

Millennials crave *inclusion*—especially younger Millennials, who grew up judging themselves on how many "likes" or "loves" their photos received. We must let them know that their opinions matter and are valued within our companies—especially where staffing is involved.

How to Get More From Your Millennial Workers

Drop your own negativity to get more from your Millennial workers. Deleting any negativity is *key* for building a Millennial-friendly corporate culture. This generation feeds on *inspiration, motivation, and possibility.*

If we're constantly complaining with doom-and-gloom corporate projections, we're going to miss out on the best that our Millennial workers can offer us. So much so that I'm *constantly* referring back to a few mantras (or, as some might call them, clichés): "Where there's a will there's a way" and "There's an exception to every rule."

Now listen, I know that we don't live in Lalaland, and things can get tough; it's our job to weed out the unnecessary chaos and negativity.

John Stapleton is my gut-check buddy. When we lost a big pitch, I let out all the steam I needed to in his office, knowing that he'd keep it to himself. *For my team, on the other hand, I focused only on positivity, possibility, and inspiration.* Of course, we discussed the lost business, but not with any "woe is me" undertones.

Instead, I focused on the lessons learned, the things we could improve upon, and how the open space in our client roster left a place for an even better client than the one we lost. With any loss, it's important to be transparent, but we can frame it in a way where we're highlighting anything positive that may come from the situation. This group *has* to be able to see the big picture, and it's our job to help paint it. That picture might not always be rainbows and sunshine, but Millennials will be a lot more receptive when we talk about the things we did that were mistakes and will do better in the future. How did each Millennial contribute to the big picture? This feedback is vital.

Resiliency depends on the age of the Millennial. Those on the older end of the spectrum (born in the early '80s) really had the rug pulled out from under them. They did *everything* they were told to do: "Work hard, get a degree, work your way up the ladder" only to be hit with a massive recession and tossed to the curb. These older Millennials are more cynical and less trusting than younger Millennials.

Younger Millennials were in college during the Great Recession. They had a few years for the economy to bounce back before they were on the employment scene. They don't feel as betrayed as the older Millennials and tend to be quicker to bounce back from criticism or disappointment. Nonetheless, we need to keep our negativity at bay as we build our Millennial-friendly corporate culture.

To create a culture where Millennials feel *safe*, we must model *resilience* and *tenacity*. These are the two areas in which Millennials tend to falter. Keep in mind, our Generation X and Boomer culture modeled infidelity and disloyalty for them. With the 2008 recession, we showed Millennials that our corporate culture is ruthless. If we can reverse that impression and model for our Millennial workers that we are committed to the company's success, ***and that they are an included part of that success***, we will earn their trust and can begin to capitalize on their innate abilities. If we can show them how to bounce back from trials and stay persistent, we will be one step closer to harnessing their continued creativity and ingenuity within our organizations.

Practicing What You Preach

Millennials hate hypocrisy.

So we must set high standards, live by them, and admit our faults or setbacks as we experience them. This means we must tolerate only A-team players. Even one C-team player will poison the well. We'll talk more at the end of this book about a no-tolerance policy for subpar recruits and discuss how you can help them exit stage left gracefully.

Remember that if we want our teams to be full of stars, then we must also shine brightly. We must set an example that we ourselves can live up to consistently.

Mastering the Art of the "Fly By"

In-person connections are key to get the most out of the Millennial workforce. Especially for the younger Millennials, who grew up chained to their phones, face-to-face conversations make them feel needed and appreciated in a whole new way.

When we take the time to physically walk by their desks or spend even a mere five minutes in their office, we're showing Millennials that they **matter.** We're giving them respect and recognition, and they'll give it right back to us. In-person communications are a nonnegotiable aspect of company culture.

RETENTION AS A BYPRODUCT OF COMPANY CULTURE

Later in the book, I'll provide more strategies for retaining top Millennial talent. But retention is also a byproduct of creating and implementing a company culture where Millennials feel understood and appreciated.

An example from 22squared is our series of regular GIF-offs. Millennials are obsessed with GIFs, those little animated texts we can send back and forth. In my company, whenever anyone does something commendable, we send a congratulatory message with a GIF. That message gets forwarded to someone else with another GIF, and so on, and so on! We all laugh a lot, and the Millennial being recognized feels seen and heard in her own language.

Our Millennial workers stick with us because we at 22squared take concrete actions to include *their* preferred methods of communication—like GIFs!—in our company culture.

A good corporate culture will ensure consistent recruitment of the Millennials who are the right fit *and repulsion of the ones who might sink the ship*.

Sure, it's tough to say goodbye to employees. But if someone wants to leave, I let them. Many Millennials also feel compelled to get job offers in order to get a raise or for you to match them. It's *essential* that we establish a "do not negotiate with terrorists" mentality about matching offers. If they get an offer, let them go on their way.

Retention in itself is not a strategy. It is the byproduct of a standout company culture.

FOCUSING ON MULTIPLE CULTURES TO MAKE CULTURE EASIER

My friend Evan LaPointe has started several businesses, including an analytics technology company that was acquired by Adobe and went on to be the fourth largest of its kind on the internet. He later led innovation in Adobe's Experience Cloud business, and today, he teaches enterprise-scale companies how to build cultures that naturally innovate and deliver, almost automatically identify incredible leaders (and avoid terrible ones), and are change-ready, rather than change-averse.

Evan's secret to success? He sees businesses as having many cultures, not just one. Evan begins with the bedrock culture of value creation: what does our organization do to create real value for the outside world, such that the outside world creates value for us? A remarkably small number of companies can clearly articulate this idea in plain English. If you can't clearly state how you create real value for your customers, Millennials can smell the lack of empathy for the outside world. They will disconnect from value creation and will use their vivid imaginations to picture the many varieties of failure that might lie in your future.

Millennials will steer clear of your organization, knowing it'll be them on the chopping block when things go sideways. And even before that happens, they don't want to tell their friends that they work for a company that doesn't create honest value for anyone but itself.

Now, in practical terms, let's imagine we *do* have this well-articulated. Is it going to be easier or harder to come up with marketing messaging when we know how we create value for people? Easier or harder to iterate our product or innovate? Easier or harder to allow for autonomy when our people are on the same page about this? Easier or harder to inspire and keep engagement? How about identifying the people and teams who managed not only to contribute significantly this quarter, but also to the big picture?

It doesn't take much Googling to see that companies today are badly struggling with every one of these things. Next, you'll need to examine your culture of getting real work done. The modern company is in a constant state of executing across the organization, not within silos. To most, this means a tangled mess of dependencies, sequences, and process, but not to the best, says Evan.

"The idea that a department or person has 'internal clients' is one of the worst ideas in the workplace today," Evan remarks. "All this does is breed the same kind of issues we see in any other client relationship: unreasonable expectations and timelines, hurried and unclear communication (while making you feel bad for asking for more information), a total inability to admit weaknesses or fear, and often what feels like a complete lack of respect for your time, other priorities, or personal values. When's the last time you saw the client/provider relationship of a stock broker, insurance company, landscaping company, or wedding cake baker and said, 'Boy, if we could only mimic that relationship everywhere throughout our company, we'd be set!"

Evan concludes with one tidy math equation: CLIENTS = ATTITUDE. "Our conversations aren't about substance and learning," he says. "They're about dependencies and blame and resentment."

So, no, the notion of internal dependencies and tossing work over the fence as an internal client is not leading to great cultures.

What's the alternative?

Evan says it's a culture of perspectives. While he was building that software company that was later acquired by Adobe, he knew that everyone's individual opinions and knowledge were not enough to build a product that would win in an ultracompetitive marketplace. "We had to have two things going full-tilt: better ideas than our competitors, and a faster pace at the same time," he says. "We were bootstrapped; our two closest competitors had raised over $110 million in venture funding, and we were also competing with Google's and Adobe's products. It was a David vs. Goliath vs. another Goliath story."

So they built a "super brain" by making sure every idea owner proactively tapped sales, marketing, engineering, design, product, and customer voice. It was not a top-down organization because the top simply doesn't know as much about reality. "We originally did it to boost idea quality, but something interesting happened: it made us faster," says Evan. "Not a little bit faster, either. Dramatically faster. This was all because the super brain understood what the market wanted, exactly how it would look and function, exactly how we would go about building it, and there was total trust."

This approach also had this other amazing benefit: choosing leaders was "stupidly simple," says Evan. If a person clearly had a positive effect on ideas, decisions, engagement, and adaptability, they were in. If someone had a negative effect on any of these things, no chance. "That's all a leader's job is, yet we see so many leaders who clearly diminish others' ideas, rush decisions, kill engagement, and are less flexible than an iron rod," he says. "Today, we call this impact Intangible Value, and it's completely measurable and actionable at scale."

The simplest way to author this culture is to actually author a separate culture for each group, department, or function. When the team culture will detail the kind of work it does, its standards for quality, communication, and other aspects; it ends with a list of the perspectives the group uniquely has (things only sales, for example, can know) and a list of the perspectives the group needs to dramatically increase idea and decision quality.

Bringing all of these written cultures together form a sort of "marketplace" filled with trusting relationships. "It's almost magic," Evan says.

There are many other cultures, but the last one Evan insisted on discussing is the culture of thought. Put simply, what approach to thinking do we believe yields the best ideas and decisions?

This is the one that upsets the apple cart of tradition the most. The simple fact is that the greatest intelligence does not lie at the top of the large organization today. It is in the middle of the organization, and our culture has to not only declare this as truth, it also has to back it up with action.

Wait . . . who is that we see in the middle of the organization? The ones talking to customers and selling every day? The ones writing all of the code? The ones handling issues? The ones who have to deal with the aftermath of imperfect strategies? You guessed it: bunches of Millennials.

"For senior leaders, their most valuable tools today are their ears," says Evan. "Leaders who listen intensely to the middle of the organization walk away with better ideas, fuel for better strategies and decisions, and more real-world information on how plans look in reality. They'd inherently gain buy-in, engagement, and adaptability simply because they are showing they give a damn."

Just in case you're thinking it: no, your org chart is not designed for this. "That's like saying a waterfall is built to carry water upward and across a mountain," says Evan. "The technology of hierarchical organizations was invented for a very specific purpose, and it needs help when it comes to ideation, decision making, innovation, and listening to the middle of the org. History answers this claim pretty clearly."

Larger organizations will have to buy or invent the technology and approaches to accomplish this kind of listening at scale, but when they see how much this accelerates pace and improves quality of ideas and decisions, any fears of this slowing us all down begin to fade away.

The easiest way to reconnect with reality is to listen to those who are in reality. For most companies, the opinion of a person who flew on a private jet within the last 30 days may be interesting, but it is probably not even remotely the most accurate opinion when it comes to what the market needs, how things should be designed or built, or what estimation of cost, effort, or emotional response will go along with execution. That all comes from the super brain . . . often from your Millennial team members. And not only is this super brain smart . . . it also loves being used.

Whether you choose to look at culture as a large, multifaceted phenomenon or as an ecosystem of separate but interconnected elements as described here is up to you. What Evan highlights in our conversations together and in his business is that it's most important to understand that culture is only real when you see it being actively used during real work. Yeah, you can have food trucks and movies on the lawn to supplement relationships, but the real relationships form *in* the work, not in between the work. This is the deficiency of the older approaches of mission statements and core values: people are either too embarrassed or too disenfranchised with these things to dare bring them up in a meeting or conversation. Evan says it this plainly: "If your culture can't be used verbatim in a meeting, and isn't used in most meetings, it simply isn't real . . . it's just stuff printed on a wall or a distant memory of bowling."

QUICK SUMMARY

- Transparency and purpose-driven initiatives create a company culture to help Millennials thrive.

- Diversity is a primary concern of Millennials and a major influence on improving work product and client relationships. If you're not proactively doing something about diversity and inclusion, you're way behind.

- Millennials are incredibly concerned with feelings. They want and need to sense that they are appreciated. We should make them the heroes of our organization and position us leaders as guides to help them achieve their best versions of themselves. We must let them know their opinions matter and are valued within our companies.

- Create a culture of resiliency by staying positive during even the most difficult times. Show Millennials how to bounce back from trials and stay persistent. Remember: resiliency depends on the age of the Millennial. Those on the older end of the spectrum (born in the early '80s) really had the rug pulled out from under them. They did *everything* they were told to do: "Work hard, get a degree, work your way up the ladder" only to be hit with a massive recession and tossed to the curb. These older Millennials are more cynical and less trusting than younger Millennials. Younger Millennials were in college during the Great Recession. They had a few years for the economy to bounce back before they were on the employment scene. They don't feel as betrayed as the older Millennials and tend to be quicker to bounce back from criticism or disappointment.

- Millennials hate hypocrisy. If we want our teams to be full of stars, then we must also shine brightly. We must set an example that we ourselves can live up to consistently.

- Master the art of the "fly by." When we take the time to physically walk by their desks or spend even a mere five minutes in their office, we're showing Millennials that they matter. We're giving them respect and recognition, and they'll give it right back to us.
- Cultivate a Millennial-friendly company culture, and you'll retain your Millennial workforce.
- Embrace multiple cultures within your company.

MAKE IT HAPPEN.

Creating a company culture that attracts the "right" kind of Millennials is one of the most important things we can do to ensure the longevity and success of our organization. Here are some key suggestions to help us craft the type of workplace that will bring in our ideal Millennial employees:

1. Hero your people.
2. Permit your Millennial team members to help craft the culture.
3. Delete your negative attitude.
4. Set high standards—and then make sure *you* live by them, too.
5. Master the art of the fly by.
6. Remember that retention is a byproduct of a stellar company culture.
7. Use this simple 5-Point model to develop your company culture. Make sure that you establish guidelines around how your organization deals with each of these critical questions:
   A. How will you treat each other?
   B. How will you act within the group?
   C. How will you deal with the negative things?

    D. How will you connect with your team?

    E. How will you connect your team with each other?

I'm giving you access to exclusive Millennial Whisperer bonus resources that will help you craft a Millennial-friendly company culture. To check out these valuable tools, and much more, go to TheMillennialWhisperer.com/BookResources.

And if you want a sneak peek before you head to the resource hub, here's a sample of what you'll find there:

1. Team Vision Statement
2. Ideal Meeting Agendas
3. Purpose Plans
4. My Own Sweet 16 Rules
5. Social media marketing guide: How to show the world that you're not a stodgy, old organization but one that actually celebrates its employees instead.
6. Additional plug-and-play templates to make culture creation a cinch.

CHAPTER 2

ATTRACTING THE RIGHT MILLENNIALS

Giving Your Company and Your Millennial Team Members a Built-In Advantage

Tyler Hartsook is one of our top Millennial employees at 22squared. Scratch that. He's one of our top employees, period.

Know how long it took to make him part of our team?

Six years.

Tyler and my college roommate used to shoot hoops together, and we first connected socially about a decade ago. I liked Tyler's energy. We stayed in touch via email and FB messenger and kept running into each other in the city, but that was the extent of our interaction.

Tyler was brilliant at content marketing and strategy but was also a nontraditional student with a bit of a chip on his shoulder. About six years ago, he approached me asking about working at 22squared, and I told him he wasn't ready.

That was that for a while, and Tyler took a position at an old-school agency. He's compared the experience to advertising boot camp, but he thrived in that pressure-filled atmosphere.

I observed his success from the outside for about a year, seeing the chip drop from his shoulder, before approaching him about making a move to 22squared. He turned me down.

We did this dance—back and forth—for another three years or so. I watched Tyler grow and mature into the type of leader who'd be able to run my whole Atlanta department at 22squared someday and, about a year ago, I approached him again.

It wasn't an easy decision for Tyler. At his other agency, he had great benefits, a solid salary, and a stellar reputation. He was risking a lot to come work with us. But because we had been "flirting" for years, Tyler had a chance to observe 22's vision and mission in action.

When asked why he made the jump to our agency, Tyler pointed out that he saw the pride we take in nurturing our employees and helping them find their own passions. More than just a paycheck, he said, we offer our Millennial employees a sense of purpose.

Tyler has achieved every goal, and then some.

Here's the thing. If I had hired Tyler years ago when he first approached me, it wouldn't have worked. We were different people. Both of us needed to grow and evolve to get to the place where we could create opportunities for each other.

Tyler's story shows us that once we've recognized Millennials as one of our greatest assets and have created a culture that will help them feel inspired and appreciated, we can learn how to attract the *right* Millennials, and this chapter provides the right strategies.

Certainty in Uncertain Times

So, what are Millennials looking for in a place where they're willing to spend their time, effort, and energy?

The data shows that Millennials want *longevity*. Yes, longevity. Those older Millennials who went from AOL to LOL in a blink of an eye? Yeah, they jumped ship time and again—in the past. The reality is so much has changed in the past 10 years. Millennials feel massive uncertainty due the news they are reading on their social channels and the political climate within what appears to be a divided country. They are seeking somewhere to grow.

Now more than ever, with so much noise in the marketplace, and so many distractions, Millennials desire *meaning* and *purpose* in their work, as well as *variety* so that they stay engaged with the jobs we've given them.

And now that we've begun to craft a company culture that speaks to these Millennial "must-haves," we've given ourselves a leg up on the competition when it comes to recruiting new talent into our organization.

Sure, plenty of Millennial candidates are entitled and lazy . . . but guess what? The same was true 10 and 20 years ago; we just called them "bad candidates" or "underperforming employees."

It shocks me how many businesses are quick to hire and slow to fire. It should be the opposite. We must have the right people in the right places on our teams to make the kind of impact we desire to make, and this doesn't just happen by chance. It's also absolutely *critical* that employees take the courtship of Millennials into their own hands instead of just relying on an HR Department. Candidates need to see the full picture and get to know their potential role outside of the parameters that normal interviewing follows.

Why do we continue to sell our companies to candidates? They know what they want. Instead, I end every interview with, "I'm not going to try to sell you on why you should be at 22squared—you need to feel like you *want* to be here. If not, then no big deal!"

(This is much easier to say than do, and it took me at least five years to figure out. Not surprisingly, I had shorter-term employees who would last only a year or two.)

We need a long period of recruitment, and a deep understanding of what Millennials want, to attract top-quality Millennial talent for the next level of success.

For example, Jeff McManus, author of *Growing Weeders into Leaders* (Morgan James Publishing), is the Director of Landscape Services at the University of Mississippi (among other roles). In other words, he's the head of landscaping there. He learned that 62% of students who visit a college campus make a decision about whether they will attend that college within a matter of minutes. He also learned the most important factor that impacts that decision is how the campus looks—the buildings and the landscaping. Jeff shares this information with his team along with the message that the buildings of the University of Mississippi are filled with the next generation of doctors, engineers, and creators. Their lawn work might attract the doctor who cures cancer to their school, or the next great building designer, or a Nobel Prize winner in literature. It's no surprise Ole' Miss wins so many awards for most beautiful campus. Their team is motivated to go their best work because they understand the big purpose behind their lawn mowing, trash collecting, and tree trimming. And that has created a look and feel to their campus that makes Millennials want to attend Ole' Miss.

Now, for the flip side. Almost every single one of our recruits at 22squared goes through a freelance-to-hire scenario (especially entry-level candidates). We test drive potential employees for four to six weeks before giving them an offer of employment. *Only 25 percent of people make it through and become hires, showing just how important it is to observe someone's interactions before making him or her a full-time employee.*

And even prior to the freelance-to-hire stage, we're courting the Millennials who catch our eye. We'll meet them on their own turf for casual interviews or arrange for other Millennial team members to take them to lunch.

Just like building any quality relationship, the Millennial recruitment period is an investment that will pay long-term dividends.

HOW TO BUILD LONG-TERM RELATIONSHIPS WITH MILLENNIAL EMPLOYEES

In 2011 and 2012, PwC, the University of Southern California, and the London Business School surveyed more than 44,000 employees around the world, discovering six key learnings:

1. Many Millennial employees are unconvinced that excessive work demands are worth the sacrifices to their personal lives.

2. Millennials say that creating a strong cohesive, team-oriented culture at work and providing opportunities for interesting work—including assignments around the world—are important to their workplace happiness, even more so than their non-Millennial counterparts.

3. Many—but not all—stereotypes about Millennials are untrue.

4. Millennial attitudes are not *totally* universal, although there is significant commonality between the United States/Canada and Western Europe.

5. While the same basic drivers of retention exist for both Millennials and non-Millennials, their relative importance varies, with Millennials placing a greater emphasis on being supported and appreciated.

Millennials are looking for personal growth and development. They really want to be part of organizations where they can move forward in a personal *and* a professional capacity.

The PwC study found that, as leaders, it's crucial that we "get the 'deal' right" to attract top Millennial talent. In other words, Millennials want to make sure that their work environment actually matches up to what we as leaders tell them it will be like on the front end. So, for example, flexible working arrangements or policies such as unlimited vacation time should actually match up with how we present these "benefits." If we promote unlimited vacation time to a potential employee without explaining that his work needs to be handled by agreeable coworkers during his absence, and then he becomes frustrated that he can't take his "unlimited" vacation while his coworkers are also on holiday, that's a miscommunication that we could have avoided at the outset.

We must clearly explain and define our company culture and policies *prior* to making an employment offer. Remember that this generation can veer toward the cynical, so we must follow through on the perks we promise.

The PwC NextGen Study also found that 96% of Millennials want to talk face-to-face about career plans and progress. "Increase transparency around compensation, rewards, and career decisions," write the authors. "Take the mystery out of compensation decisions, and provide greater transparency to employees regarding their career development. Create a meaningful rewards structure that regularly acknowledges both large and small contributions made by employees. Build a sense of community. Emphasize teamwork, appreciation and support from supervisors, and give employees honest, real time feedback, face-to-face." As we recruit Millennial talent, we must communicate our commitment to developing their skills and talents. *An annual review is not sufficient for a Millennial.* We can consider monthly or at least quarterly reviews for our Millennial hires, and we can let them know during the interview phase that they'll have the opportunity to get regular performance check-ins so they can course-correct quickly if needed.

(Coincidentally, on our whiteboard, I've written, "EVERY DAY IS A PERFORMANCE REVIEW.)"

The more we communicate with our potential employees on the front end, the better. Millennials don't want to be micromanaged, but unlike Generation Xers and Boomers, many of them never worked until they were out of college. They don't want someone constantly looking over their shoulder, but they love receiving specialized training that will help them do their jobs more effectively.

Work as a "Thing" not a "Place"

Additionally, to attract the best Millennials into our companies, we need to be willing to contribute to their personal and professional goals. As I mentioned earlier, we can give them autonomy in ways they crave, such as flex time. We can also consider giving them diversity and variety by allowing them to work overseas if your company has an international presence: the PwC Study found that 37% of Millennials see working overseas as part of their career path.

Flexibility also emerged as a critical way to attract top Millennial talent. According to the PwC study, 66% of Millennials want to shift their work hours. "Millennials do not believe that productivity should be measured by the number of hours worked at the office," write the authors, "but by the output of the work performed. They view work as a 'thing' and not a 'place.'" I tell all employees in my group that there are rules, but you do as you please, and I won't question your whereabouts or working from home. (We'll discuss more about flex time later in this book.) Once again, we've got to protect this house.

Personality Over Pedigree

As we look for the Millennial workers who will become the core of our workforce during the coming decades, we must consider personality and adaptability over pedigree and accomplishments.

My friend Nick tells a story of when he was a practicing New York City attorney. He was involved in his prestigious firm's hiring process, and a law student at a prestigious university landed in his office for an interview. This student—we'll call him Jason—was, despite his academic achievement, the exact type of Millennial we all want to *avoid* bringing into our company.

Fortunately for Nick, Jason showed his true colors in the initial interview. In fact, Jason spent his precious minutes with Nick *reversing* the interview process and asking Nick to explain why the student should choose Nick's firm instead of others.

Nick suggested to his colleagues that hiring Jason was the wrong move, and Jason's own actions backed up Nick's warning. After the interview, Jason sent Nick a list of his employment offers and asked Nick to sell him on why his firm would be a better choice for Jason than other firms. Nick again told his colleagues he didn't believe Jason to be the right fit for the firm, although he and the firm gave Jason the benefit of the doubt and committed to completing the interview process. In the end, Jason strung Nick's firm along for months before ultimately accepting a position with a rival firm. Nick was relieved, but the law firm wasted months courting a mismatched recruit.

I had a similar experience at 22squared. During our "doing the dance" hiring process, one particular recruit stood out: I'll call him Adam (to protect his identity). I saw something special in him and lobbied *hard* to get the firm to issue him an offer.

I'll never forget being on vacation in Watercolor, Florida, with my family and getting a frantic message from a coworker that Adam really needed to speak with me. I reluctantly relaxed my boundaries and took the call. I'm glad I did because it helped me realize Adam wasn't a good match for our culture. I'll save the details, but essentially Adam wanted several concessions and guarantees we couldn't make. It immediately became clear that Adam would not have been a good fit with the culture at 22squared, so we agreed to go our separate ways.

But our lengthy recruitment process actually let me build the type of relationship with him where he felt comfortable enough to have this frank discussion before it was too late. The time I invested on the front end to give him a real chance to fit into the organization was well spent. Hiring a mismatched employee is much more expensive than having a position open longer. While it was disappointing that it didn't work out, our lengthy recruitment process let us find that out before he signed a contract and we committed to him as a team member. So, we must work to avoid the wrong candidates as hard as we work to recruit the right ones.

Empowering Our Teams During the Hiring Process

Perhaps the first interview occurs in a coffee shop—a place where most Millennials feel at home. If a potential recruit passes the first round of interviews, then it's time to bring our current Millennial employees into the equation.

Peer-to-peer interviews will make the people we've already hired feel like they have a say in who their newest colleague will be, and the potential hire will feel like his or her opinions will be valued inside our company because it's clear that we're already including Millennials in big decisions like hiring.

Remember that when we include Millennials in our hiring process, it doesn't mean they have any kind of *final* say. But the mere fact that we let them do a drive-by of potential new employees will build their sense of contribution in our companies.

Bringing Leaders on Board to Attract the Best

Remember how important it is for Millennials to have an inspirational leader? It's one of the three top things—along with transparency and autonomy—that they must have to flourish in any work environment. When we have an inspirational leader instead of a mid-level manager do the interviewing, we will quickly weed out the "wrong" Millennials. Better yet, the "right" ones will be completely sold on our company before we ever even make an offer.

Freelance to Hire

Our new employees will spend the majority of their waking hours within our organization. This is a much bigger decision than some hiring teams act like it is. A freelance-to-hire process allows us and our Millennial prospects to see what it would really be like to work together before a full commitment is made. We get to prove ourselves to each other. If we can't convince entry-level candidates to do a freelance-to-hire model, then we probably have to revisit our overall culture in general as it's a sign that we've got bigger problems (and we ought to check those Glassdoor ratings).

There's a mutual respect implied here that speaks to a Millennial's need to feel valued and appreciated.

As leaders, we can present this opportunity as a win-win, because it is. They get to test drive our companies and make sure that our offices are a place where they can do work that's purpose-filled and stimulating. We get to observe them closely over a period of time to assure ourselves that they're really the right fit for our organization. With an attractive freelance-to-hire offer, we can capitalize on Millennials' desire to know that they're working somewhere they can feel proud of and that allows their passions to flourish and their motivations met.

Hire slow, fire fast. We've heard it before, but we've done the opposite and lived to regret it. A solid onboarding system will help integrate our new employees into our existing culture. Ideally, we'd observe them closely during a minimum of the first month of their engagement so that we can tackle any issues that arise.

The "North Star" Principles

Developing a written corporate purpose statement that includes a few "North Star" principles will make it easier for the "right" Millennials to find their home and for the "wrong" Millennials to show themselves the door.

At 22squared, we tell everyone they must do three things if they expect to have a future with us:

A. Be willing to put the organization in front of yourself and your own ego.

B. Always be willing to get your hands dirty no matter what the ask is.

C. Have a can-do attitude. See the opportunities instead of the obstacles.

When we are clear on our company's values, we'll attract Millennials who are excited to contribute to our vision. We've created a Millennial Leadership Assessment that will assess these and the other cultural factors based on extensive data about Millennials in the workplace. Claim your free Millennial Leadership Assessment on the Resources page at TheMillennialWhisperer.com/BookResources.

Speaking to Millennials in Their Language

Millennials are a *connected* generation. They are quick to Google search and fact-check online. So, we must keep company initiatives in place that will keep our rankings high on sites such as Glassdoor and Indeed.

We also need to be paying attention to our social media presence and the platforms we're active on. We can consider our community initiatives—how will Millennials take notice? Old-guard charities can give way to organizations we can support that draw the attention of a younger crowd. Posts about the company's purpose and broader outreach should accompany posts about Happy Hours and other events—let's make it worth Millennials' time.

A Sticky Subject: Courting on Social Media

This is a somewhat controversial approach, but it's an essential ingredient to building up relationships. We'll talk about using social media to build relationships with Millennial employees who already work for you. But social media is also effective for identifying and recruiting Millennial candidates to fill current needs or build relationships for future ones.

Social media can bring about great relationships—with the right parameters. When done well, it can be a useful recruitment tool, allowing us to connect with potential employees who show themselves on social media to have relevant interests or talents.

For example, as simple as it sounds, you might find it useful to join industry Facebook or LinkedIn groups or follow relevant hashtags on Twitter or Instagram. You'll find people being helpful, sharing stories, and even demonstrating interest by following and posting about relevant news stories. Tyler and I had been Facebook friends for years before he came on board. We developed a digital relationship first before becoming in-person friends.

Social media courting can work in any industry, too. Looking for marketing help for a law firm? Follow relevant hashtags, such as #LegalMarketing, or search for key terms, such as law firm marketing, lawyer marketing, or attorney marketing. You'll find posts from agencies if you're looking to outsource and in-house marketing professionals at law firms sharing updates from posts they're reading, content they're creating, or conferences they're attending. Get to know the people posting using those hashtags. Share their content, like, etc. They'll notice, and you can learn useful information while you build relationships with potential employees.

Want help with digital marketing? Join relevant digital marketing Facebook groups. Get to know people in there. See who is most knowledgeable and helpful. Search social media posts and profiles for key terms relating to positions you're looking to fill or may need to fill in the future. As with hashtag following, you'll get to know potential candidates for future openings while learning useful information about the subject.

One warning: Stalking candidates on Facebook, Instagram, Snapchat or Tinder (kidding) only spells trouble. I'm not suggesting we use social media to be creepy or cross any lines, so we need to be careful. But with so much public content being shared, social media gives us an unprecedented ability to search, follow, and connect with potential candidates based on the content they share in posts, using hashtags, or in groups.

Recently, I was in Manhattan with a colleague and we met with a "friend" who'd been working at Facebook for years. This friend and I were in a closed Facebook group together and had never actually met in real life. I gave him a big hug and asked how his new baby was. My colleague asked, "How long have you guys known each other?" I admitted, with embarrassment, that we'd never met in real life. Our whole relationship had been built via instant messages and social media. Still, we can develop courtships effectively on social media. Twitter and LinkedIn are fairly open platforms, and more advice on building effective relationships on social media can be found at TheMillennialWhisperer. com/BookResources.

QUICK SUMMARY

- Once we've reorganized Millennials as one of our greatest assets, and once we've created a culture that will help them feel inspired and appreciated, the next step is to learn how to attract the right Millennials to our company.

- Businesses should be quick to fire and slow to hire. At 22squared, we play out a freelance-to-hire scenario. We test drive employees for four to six weeks before giving them an offer of employment. We clearly define our company culture and policies prior to making an employment offer. A freelance-to-hire process allows us and our Millennial prospects to see what it would really be like to work together before a full commitment is made. We get to prove ourselves to each other.

- As we look for the Millennial workers who will become the core of our workforce during the coming decades, we must consider personality and adaptability over pedigree and accomplishments. We must avoid the candidates who, instead of harnessing passions to drive themselves, are driven by title and salary.

- Empower your team during the hiring process by involving them. Peer-to-peer interviews will make the people we've already hired feel like they have a say in who their newest colleague will be. The potential client will also feel like his or her opinions will be valued inside our company because it's clear that we're already including Millennials in big decisions like hiring. They don't have the final say, necessarily, but it'll build their sense of contribution in our companies.

- Social media is an effective tool for identifying and recruiting Millennial candidates. It allows us to connect with potential employees who show themselves to have relevant interests or talents.

—— MAKE IT HAPPEN. ——

Recruiting Millennials can be an ongoing process that our current Millennial workers participate in alongside us. Giving our current staff a say in the people they'll sit beside at the office also has the added benefit of solidifying company culture and improving retention rates.

To recruit Millennials who will be true team players and enhance our efforts, we must remember to employ these strategies:

1. Make sure our leaders—not just our managers—do the interviewing.
2. "Do the dance."
3. Consider a freelance-to-hire process.
4. Use digital resources to mold our reputation.
5. Streamline our recruitment process by developing hard success principles within our company.
6. Give constant feedback within our onboarding process.

CHAPTER 3

GETTING AND KEEPING MILLENNIALS ENGAGED

Unlocking the Power of Such a Passionate and Resourceful Generation

Awkward! That's how one very talented Millennial was behaving at a global security company. Its leaders understand that Millennial employees are integral to the company's continued positive impact, but there was this particular individual who was socially awkward within the corporate environment.

I asked a Senior HR Business Partner at this company, whom we'll call Darcy, *how* he was able to unlock the potential of this key Millennial recruit.

Darcy emphasized that this particular employee was the most knowledgeable subject-matter expert (a/k/a SME) to interact with the company's customers around a certain program. This employee's role required him to liaise with customers often and demanded the highest level of professionalism.

At the start, the employee seemed to be the perfect fit. He participated in a client call and was praised for his deep understanding of the customer's needs.

But things began to unravel just one week later. The same employee made contact with the same customer, yet was rude and unprofessional to such an extent that the customer requested an apology from the executive team and a change in the company's representation on the customer's account.

Darcy was tasked with investigating the situation and deciding whether or not to initiate disciplinary proceedings against the employee.

Darcy's conversation with the employee revealed that he was "a genius . . . who had no coaching or guidance on how to navigate corporate America. He displayed all the traits of a Millennial: he wanted his opinion to be heard, he wanted to work when he felt like working. He wanted a bigger challenge."

Recognizing that this employee could not easily be replaced and that he needed mentorship to succeed at the company, Darcy took it upon himself to coach the Millennial. He recommended learning courses that would develop the employee's skills. He met with the Millennial regularly. He affirmed his team member's knowledge of the subject matter at issue while also being candid with him about his lack of communication skills being the biggest hindrance to his career.

The outcome? Darcy relayed that the employee made "a complete turnaround." The Millennial apologized sincerely to the displeased customer and was welcomed back onto the project.

Darcy found that he also grew from the experience of "rehabbing" this particular employee. He notes that it would have been much easier to render a disciplinary course of action for this employee and just move on, but that would only have created more frustrations for the employee.

It could have led easily to the employee feeling undervalued and quitting, which would have meant a scramble for the company to find a new team member. At a minimum, taking disciplinary action against this employee would have hindered productivity and cost the company both time and money.

Darcy emphasized that it's important for leaders to make the effort to understand Millennial employees' situations and show empathy toward them while also deciding upon the mutually beneficial type of relationship they can maintain so that all parties can move forward. It's a perfect example of Millennials engaged.

WHEN THE REAL WORK BEGINS

To review some key points:
- Millennials desire constant feedback.
- Millennials want to have purposeful work and feel challenged in their vocation.
- Millennials must feel their opinions are valued before they'll give us their best.

Getting Millennials Engaged

We must get our Millennials engaged. And then we must keep them engaged. It can be a tough task, especially with the younger Millennials who grew up attached to their electronic devices (*don't forget that this is actually the fault of the older generations—iPads on the road trip, parents?*). But we can do it—and we must, unless we want all our efforts up to this point to go to waste.

The key is building quality relationships at many different levels, and this chapter explains how to do it. But because relationship building is an art, not a science, there's plenty of flexibility to color outside the lines of these solutions and strategies.

Let's ask a better question. It's a good lesson for us leaders to nurture our Millennial talent by being willing to veer away from the traditional HR corrective measures.

When a Millennial employee's performance needs review, let's ask a better question. Rather than asking, "How can I get this person to fall in line?" we need to start asking, "How can I understand this person so that I'm able to equip him to succeed?"

Millennials need autonomy *within* structure. They do best with a consistent feedback loop, and for feedback to be effective, they need to clearly understand what expectations have been set. From the top leadership to the entry-level employee, every worker should know what is necessary to succeed in the job. Then, as the leaders, we must make sure that each employee has a senior-level team member assigned to review these standards with him or her. We must let our Millennial employees know *quickly* if there are places where they can improve so that they can pivot and have a greater chance of success. The more they feel valued, seen, and appreciated, the better work they will do.

Not Just Satisfaction

Understanding the difference between engagement and satisfaction is one of the most important distinctions we can make as leaders, says Chandler McCormack, CEO of OxBlue, which engineers and sells a specialized camera solution used to manage and market construction projects. While employee satisfaction is important, employee *engagement* is what moves the needle at companies.

McCormack describes engagement as the what employees do with what he calls "discretionary effort." Discretionary efforts are things employees do above and beyond the bare minimum.

Satisfaction, on the other hand, only refers to whether employees are "happy."

To McCormack, the level of employee engagement is one of, if not *the* biggest factor that separates good companies from great ones.

An employee making a decent paycheck, doing *just* enough not to be a problem but nothing extraordinary, eating all your free snacks, and halfway down the stairs at 5:01 P.M. would probably show up on a satisfaction survey as "very satisfied." But they might just be going through the motions and happy to fly under the radar.

To make your company great, McCormack suggests focusing our efforts on things that improve employee engagement. When we do, we end up with both satisfied *and* engaged employees who help make our companies great. That's where success comes from.

Gallup® regularly researches employee engagement by telephone survey. It defines engaged employees as employees who are "involved in, enthusiastic about, and committed to their work and workplace."[12] According to a recent article posted on Gallup's website, "Leaders often make a mistake in their approach to engagement."[13] That mistake? Not using "shared responsibility" correctly. When leaders use shared responsibility, they build shared ownership, which helps build employee engagement.

One easy way to build shared responsibility and shared ownership is to help employees set work priorities and performance goals. Gallup's data supports the connection between helping employees set work priorities and performance goals and their level of engagement. For example, 66% of employees who were engaged workers strongly agreed that their managers helped them set work priorities. Similarly, 69% of engaged employees strongly agreed that their manager helped them set performance goals.[14]

According to research by the Aon Consulting firm (AON),[15] employee engagement levels hit an all-time high in 2017, with 65% of employees being classified as engaged across the world, 64% in the US.

The top five factors that drive engagement in North America, according to AON's research, are:

- Enabling Infrastructure
- Senior Leadership
- Rewards & Recognition (which includes "fair pay")
- Career Opportunities
- Employee Value Proposition

This tells us pay, or more specifically "fair pay," is an important factor, but not the *most* important factor when it comes to driving employee engagement. McCormack sees the same thing at OxBlue. In his words:

> Every single person we hire is at maximum engagement the day they start. From there, we whittle down their engagement through lack of clarity, lack of appreciation, limiting autonomy to much, policies that distract from what's most important, etc. A big part of our job is to keep all those engagement killers away because we can't create engagement as much as we can mess it up.
>
> At OxBlue, we don't have a dress code, pet policy, or other official policies many other companies have. When people ask why we don't have certain policies, my response is we don't need so many policies when we have built an environment of trust and support.
>
> We have an intrinsic but not written policy to respect people, focus on work and common sense, and not destroy the office. If your pet is so cute that bringing her to work shuts down half the company for the day, she pees on the floor, and barks all day, then don't bring your pet to work. We don't need a policy

just to have a policy. Having non-critical policies steals energy from things that are most important. That's just one example of not messing it up when it comes to our role in keeping that first day engagement going for years.

McCormack's experience at OxBlue suggests we all could take a hard look at our policies and question whether we could do a better job by focusing on big-picture issues, such as creating a culture of trust and support, and not the small-picture issues, such as whether someone can wear jeans on Thursday or bring pets in on Mondays.

The Loneliest Number

As connected as they appear to be on the surface, Millennials are *lonely.*

Global health services company Cigna looked into loneliness by generation in its survey of more than 20,000 adults online in the US based on the UCLA Loneliness Scale, a 20-item questionnaire developed to assess subjective feelings of loneliness or social isolation. Based on its survey, Cigna concluded loneliness in America as an "epidemic," with Millennials and the generation that follows them, Generation Z, the loneliest of all generations.[16]

A study of nearly 2,000 people ages 19 to 32 published in 2017 in the *American Journal of Preventive Medicine,* meanwhile, found that the more Millennials spend time on social media, the more likely they are to feel socially isolated.[17]

Millennials may try to mask their loneliness with the appearance of hyper-connectivity via social media. The internet has become a "virtual escape from loneliness for the younger generations."[18] One statistic shows that 88% of those ages 18–29 (an age range that encompasses the younger Millennials) use at least one social media site.[19]

So what's the effect of all this screen time? Research shows that Millennials have a tendency to judge their popularity and even their self-worth by the number of "friends" and "followers" they've amassed. An article by Leslie Haddon of the London School of Economics and Political Science found that "the number of 'friends' on social networking site profiles, including visits to those profiles and 'likes' expressed by others, were all taken to indicate popularity."[20]

Data also reveals that while increased screen time may lead to a rise in depression and even suicide, people who spend more time having "face-to-face social interactions" can decrease their risk of those incredibly negative outcomes.[21] Instead, I encourage employees to ditch their ruthless pursuit of the perfect selfie and perfection as a whole and to embrace a bit of the chaos that is life. (Just wait for my *A River Runs Through It* story later in this book.)

Because of this loneliness, Millennials also crave stability. They've seen so many things change so quickly around them during their formative years, and all this change combined with their feelings of isolation can cause high levels of unrest.

Millennials want a place to hang their hat. They want to be part of a workplace where they can contribute—and where they feel valued, appreciated, and understood.

If we focus on giving our Millennial employees attention, focused training, constructive feedback, and positive affirmation, we'll build a team with staying power.

Giving a Little Love to Get Genuine Connection

To build and maintain my relationships with my Millennial employees, I've learned to get social with them. And no, I don't mean time together outside of the office, although we do have a fair amount of fun (if you can't tell by now). Instead, I've learned to meet my team on their own turf and engage with them on their social media platforms of choice.

I follow my Millennial employees on Instagram and Facebook. I watch their stories, and I make sure to hit the "like" button when they post something about their life. My wife, Julie, will sometimes look over at me while I'm on my phone and ask me what I'm doing. She's learned that if she sees me on my phone, chances are that I'm working.

Following our teams on social media—not in a creepy, stalkerish way but in the same way their actual friends do—shows that we're engaged and interested in them as people. When I see an employee post about her new puppy over the weekend and can then ask her about it back in the office, I'm building a meaningful connection. This genuine interest in their personal lives reaps tremendous benefits.

We can discover a lot about someone from social media profiles. Following and engaging with team members on social media may provides new insight into commonalities and deepens work relationships in an authentic way.

For example, if you see that one of your employees was working to construct a Habitat for Humanity house over the weekend, when you see her the next workday, you might mention a past project that you helped construct. Or you might ask another employee about the concert you noticed he attended and get curious about which song was his favorite.

Remember that younger Millennials grew up attached to their devices. Sometimes, Boomers and Gen Xers fear that they'll seem intrusive if they friend request or follow employees on FB or Instagram. For sure, don't like or comment on every post. That does seem suspect to Millennials, who want to know you care but not feel like you're watching their every move.

Statistically speaking, it takes three common passion points to connect two humans, which is not too hard to find even with the generation gap.

I encourage those who aren't convinced that following employees on social media is a great idea to try it for 30 days. An added bonus to using social media to build connection is that you get to skip the small talk and can go straight to the heart of what matters to your team members. More engagement means more profit. Trust me on this one.

Another free way to engage Millennials is to build a department or company group Facebook page. Every day someone on our team posts an article in the "22squared Content and Influencer group" about something inspirational, a cool ad campaign, or props for someone's awesome presentation. This page circumvents email and goes straight into everyone's mobile feeds.

Getting Real with Millennial Employees

I've emphasized how important transparency is to Millennials. The more we let our team members understand who we really are, flaws and all, the more they'll be willing to give.

When I first took over my team, I invited everyone over to my house for a dinner that my friend who owns a great Mexican restaurant *Verde* catered. I had my usual fall music on rotation with Rogue Wave and Bon Iver setting the tone for the evening. We sat around our giant picnic table with a fire going under our pergola and I shared a slideshow called "My Tuff Ride—a story about perseverance and resilience." (See the slides at TheMillennialWhisperer.com/BookResources.)

As I shed my own tears at some of the ups and downs and things that I had learned, my employees saw a new level of vulnerability. I told them about when I thought I was prioritizing the wrong things in life and that I thought I was drinking too much and what my bottom looked and felt like. I received a long line of hugs and many team members were a bit teary eyed. It was at this moment that the team came together for the first time.

Obviously this is an extreme example, and we all know I like extremes. A less extreme example is just admitting when you've made a mistake.

Transparency is also talking about the big picture and overcommunicating why we've made the decisions you have and standing behind them. So many leaders waver or lack the ability to put a stake down and march toward it, yet this is what Millennials *crave*. I ended my speech by talking about the importance of being a vulnerable leader and saying that we're all on a journey together and that one of the most important things everyone should do is develop a purpose for themselves and understand that this can evolve with time.

Being transparent does *not* mean giving employees total and complete honesty. They don't need to know exactly how much we take home or every single perk we receive as a leader of the company.

They do need to understand that we're human and that mistakes, rather than being grounds for discipline or dismissal, can instead be learning tools and growth opportunities.

"I cost the company hundreds of thousands of dollars."

You might expect that sentence to describe the reason someone got fired. At social media data analytics company, Unified, that sentence describes the opposite. It's part of one of the greatest success stories in company history. And it's a big reason the company has been voted one of Ad Age's and Crain's New York's "Best Places to Work."

Many companies talk about learning from their mistakes. Some of them do so in name only, as poster fodder or a shallow statement that quickly transitions a conversation into a disciplinary meeting.

But Joshua Backer, Co-Founder and Head of Operations of Unified, make this a central focus of one of the longest-standing regular operations meetings at Unified, the "Make-Good Meeting." The idea behind the Make-Good Meeting is to provide a safe space, free of fear or shame to address the inevitable mistakes that happen in the workplace.

The term "make good" refers to when advertising agencies need to return money to their clients because they didn't perform up to agreed-upon expectations. Essentially, you send back money to "make good" for your underdelivery.

As you might imagine, Unified works hard to limit "make goods," just like product manufacturers look to limit design or manufacture defects. They built sophisticated systems and processes to help prevent errors. Nonetheless, they're a service and technology provider in an emerging field with rapidly changing platforms and unique customer engagements. In that environment, there will always be occurrences of either real or perceived failures in service. For companies like Unified, those occurrences will be rare. But there's no way to eliminate them entirely.

Years ago, leadership at Unified decided they had two ways to respond to make goods: they could build a culture that responds through fear and shame or they could build one that encourages building ownership, discussion, and remediation.

After realizing years ago that this would be the case and that it would be unsustainable to have a fear or shame-based culture around inevitable mistakes, Unified chose to build ownership, discussion, and remediation of mistakes into its culture.

Unified has held Make-Good Meetings since 2013 and it's been so successful that the Millennial director who runs the meeting recently renamed it to "The Make-Good, Make Great Meeting." Even with nearly 100 employees in operations at Unified, this is one of the few mandatory meetings at the company.

During the monthly meetings, the entire Unified operations team reviews trends and individual errors. Each meeting is opened with a preamble for the new hires that this is a meeting for discussing mistakes with an eye toward transparent root-cause analysis and continuous improvement. The meeting does not allow any blame or finger-pointing. It's truly a safe place. In fact, the director who leads the meetings frequently mentions that he's been responsible for hundreds of thousands of dollars of mistakes over his six-year career at Unified. His story is particularly impactful given the fact that he's not only still *employed* by Unified, he's so valued he now gets to run the mistakes meetings.

When the meeting moves past the preamble, the team then takes turns owning their mistakes, and discussing what happened, why, what the resolution was with the customer, and how it could be avoided in the future. Some of the mistakes discussed are five-or six-figure mistakes, so they can be difficult, even emotional, for team members to discuss.

While the mistakes and resolutions discussions are incredibly valuable for the attendees, the meeting is about more than finding practical outcomes to challenges that may arise again. It's an opportunity for the entire team to witness a colleague talking through a mistake they made and how they would fix it, and then be *thanked*—yes **thanked**—by a senior leader for doing so.

PURSUING PURPOSE

Engage Millennials by allowing them to pursue their own purpose—it's up to us help them find it. We must give our Millennial employees a *personal* reason to love coming to work. They need to feel connected to something beyond the company's bottom line to make their best contributions. And no, it's not up to HR to help them find this purpose—it's our responsibility as their leader. A surprising bond is formed through this process.

At 22squared, we encourage each employee to create his or her own "purpose statement." Mine is "to inspire people and connect." My whole team knows my purpose statement, and you'd better believe that they're watching to see if I'm living it out in the way I interact with them.

I'm also setting up Jeffersonian-style dinners (where only one person at a time speaks) during which each of our employees will share his or her personal purpose statement.

Here's an excerpt from the email I sent around to my team recently (feel free to grab the template at TheMillennialWhisperer.com/BookResources and use this idea within your own organization).

Hey all,

I'll be hosting dinners in both Atlanta and Tampa where we will do a Jeffersonian dinner and everyone will present their personal purpose statement. This is your defining statement that encompasses what makes you tick (who you are), where you want to go, and why you want to do it. I'll work with each of you over the next few weeks to help hone and craft your statement. First exercise:

Create two columns. Write down everything that gives you energy in one and everything that drains your energy in the other. Let this list grow and *know there's no bad answer here.*

Then answer these:

1. **Where do you lose time?** What activities do you do that when you're doing them you forget that time exists—you forget that you're hungry and entirely consumed with the task at hand?

2. **Are you a builder or maintainer?** Do you like building new things and excel in a world of innovation and change? Or do you enjoy predictability, order, and proven constructs?

3. **If you could do one thing all day everyday what would it be?** With the exception of coming home to sleep, what job would you do ALL DAY for 14 hours? This is your time to dream.

4. **How do you want to be remembered?** In 100 years, what is it you want the world to remember about your impact?

5. **What does success look like for you?** How do you currently measure success?

REMEMBER:
Most purpose statements start with "To" and
Write in the present tense.
Choose words that Reflect Positive Action.
Keep it short.
Hit me up with any questions.
Chris

EXAMPLES:
"To inspire positive change through teaching and coaching."
"To create opportunities for today's youth."
"To encourage, engage, and equip others to believe in the possibilities."
"To positively impact the life of every person I meet."
"To encourage everyone I interact with on a daily basis."

We'll be hosting these purpose-focused dinners regularly as we onboard new team members at 22squared, because knowing this information about our staff allows us to fold purpose into their work. Consulting employees about their purpose makes leaders a part of their process and vested in their ultimate product. I wholeheartedly believe that it's essential for Millennials to understand their purpose (ideally stemming from their passions) and ensure their job matches up to it or that leaders help them find a way to evolve toward it. Encourage your Millennial team members to keep it broad and simple vs. too specific (this will come later in their careers).

Remember, Millennials crave purposeful work. When they can see that we as leaders value purpose as much as profits, we'll build yet another connection point with our team. Speaking openly about our own passions and dreams (outside of our business goals) strengthens relationships with Millennial employees.

One of the most amazing things happened when I was working with everyone on their own purposes. I realized that never in my life had I been as fulfilled as I was when helping my team find their own purpose at work. So weirdly enough, I rediscovered my own purpose through this exercise.

As a way to help our employees fulfill their purposes and in order to give back to our surrounding communities, each of our employees at 22squared receives one week of paid time off to work with his or her nonprofit of choice. Every three years, a team member gets one entire *month* off for a fully funded sabbatical. Since we instituted this policy, we've had one team member go to Nicaragua to teach lacrosse, another to Spain to work with a nonprofit, and many more take advantage of opportunities within the US.

Knowing that we as a company support what our Millennial employees care about gets and keeps them engaged.

The 70/30 Rule and the "Sitting in Your Car" Test

I have what I call my 70/30 rule for all employees. This means that 70% of your job should give you energy and get you fired up (inside your passion area). I think too many people get distracted in life by money and other pressures instead of focusing on their passions (purpose comes out of this). But the reality is 30% of your job will always kind of suck.

Millennials—and all employees—should be tattooed with this rule to avoid "the grass is always greener" complex.

We all have days when we drive to work and then just sit there for a moment, procrastinating or worrying about a big speech. That's okay. But if this pause turns to dread, if it is about the entire job and the workplace, and if it happens for more than two days in a row, then something has to change. I tell my Millennials if they experience the two-day-dread-in-the-car, I will help them find something outside of our own walls.

Upping Your EQ

That's not a typo. Emotional quotient (EQ), or emotional intelligence, is the single most important trait for navigating Millennials. A recent Forbes article by Sarah Landrum illuminates this point. "Early in 2017, the Levo Institute polled Millennials on the key elements of their career development, including the factors they credit with their personal growth. About 80% of survey respondents indicated emotional intelligence as something they actively focus on as they develop their careers," writes Sarah, who defines emotional intelligence as a person's ability to detect and recognize their own feelings and the feelings of others and respond to them in a rational way. "Additionally, a stunning 87% of Millennials in that same study revealed a strong connection between their motivation to help the company succeed and the emotional intelligence of that company's leaders."

As a firm, 22squared actually invests heavily in EQ. We have three certified Myers-Briggs Type Indicator (MBTI) trainers who issue the test and then work one-on-one with employees about what their MBTI means. We also have courses for teams to work through their overall MBTI profiles as well as those of their clients. Every year we give all employees the opportunity to take four courses. These classes build on MBTI personality type and help employees understand how to utilize

MBTI for increased communication and better understanding of people, preferences, and behavior.

- Speed Reading People
- Emotional Intelligence (EQ)
- Tipping Point
- Question Thinking

What's fascinating to me about MBTI is how it helps clarify what we know about each Millennial (and everyone else who takes the test). It gives us individual context to some of the things we know in a general sense, based on the Millennials' season of life or whether they are younger or older.

For example, we know younger Millennials grew up on technology. Based on that information alone, we might be tempted to make any younger Millennial a company's social media manager. For the purpose of this example, let's call this Millennial Paul. He's 23 years old and has had a smartphone in his hands since he was six. Chances are, Paul's more comfortable using social media than someone who was nearing retirement when Facebook debuted.

The problem with this logic is that we would be making decisions on an individual level based on information on a generational level. What if Paul's MBTI results suggest he is shy, analytical, and works better behind the scenes? He might be a good social media *analyst* but putting Paul in charge of our company's Instagram account wouldn't be putting him in a position to succeed.

If Paul was a rockstar at his main position, we could lose that rockstar to another company because we didn't take into account his individual personality style and preferences.

The impact of MBTI goes beyond assignments, too. Having a better understanding of people's personality styles and preferences on an individual level helps us understand what methods of communication will work best with each person. Some people do their best when their leaders are blunt and communicate in person. Others do their best work with checklists or email instructions.

It helps us understand how to reward and incentivize employees, too. Some people will work hard if they're incentivized with an opportunity to present a project or client pitch. Others would be terrified by that.

The blend of generational and individual understanding helps us better understand each Millennial employees and build a strong EQ. That EQ helps us make even deeper connections with our Millennial employees than we get even by understanding them on a generational level.

Seasons of life give us a broad understanding of the generation, and MBTI gives us individualized information. The two go together like donuts and coffee (even if they're vegan, non-GMO donuts and iced, half caff, ristretto, venti, four-pump, sugar-free, cinnamon, dolce soy skinny lattes in a reusable cup...).

Get a full list of resources to help increase your EQ at TheMillennialWhisperer.com/BookResources.

SHIFTING FOCUS FROM CHAMPAGNE MOMENTS TO THINGS THAT MATTER MORE

Surf clams. Sunchokes. Scallops.

These are just a few of the mouthwatering items on the multi-course tasting menu at Alinea, the world-famous Chicago restaurant run by chef Grant Achatz. When diners sit down here, however, they are not really eating—they are experiencing.

And that's because of a defining moment in Grant's life: getting diagnosed with tongue cancer a year after *Food & Wine* named him a Best New Chef. Instead of throwing in his toque, now having lost most of his taste, Grant focused on the creative presentation of his food. The result? A mind-blowing adventure in dining, one that feels more like going to the theater than a simple meal.

That was Grant's defining moment. Nobody wants tongue cancer, of course, but everybody wants a defining moment.

Let's differentiate between defining moments and champagne moments. Champagne moments are those highs following a new business win, promotion, or massive award.

Those are nice, no doubt. But champagne moments are fleeting. They come and go and if you focus too much on highs that are in many ways outside of your complete control, you become conditioned to the adrenaline rush of each one and constantly crave a bigger one. You also set yourself up for a demoralizing blow when you inevitably lose a pitch, don't get the promotion, or don't win the award.

That's why I constantly remind my Millennial team to enjoy the champagne moments but focus your attention on the ride—the small moments that make up your day or week instead of craving that champagne moment that seems to fill our Instagram feeds. This is how I used to live—from champagne moment to champagne moment but now with my Millennial team, I focus on all the small wins that will contribute to what will be *much* bigger: a defining moment.

When you focus on enjoying and investing in improving all the small things about our work week we don't need the champagne moments to keep us going. We enjoy each other and the things we do every day.

The truth is, real big moments—*defining moments*—happen only once or twice in a career, and they happen by design and chance. With the Millennial population growing so fast—no matter how long you've been in business—a defining moment awaits you. Sometimes, what we once saw as defining moments turn out not to be. We only learn then when experiences dwarf what we once believed were defining moments.

The unfortunate side is that the only one you can control is the *design* part of the equation. And guess what? Engaged Millennials hold the keys to designing defining moments. Whether it be embracing new trends and seeing ahead of the curve or just making your workplace a better and more impactful enterprise, Millennials will help design key changes in your company that lead to defining moments. You just have to empower them and encourage them on their way. But the more engaged they are, the more they'll help you design defining moments.

As you look at the *design* side of the equation to this formula, remember that's all you can control to start truly empowering your Millennial team members and putting them in a position to do their best work.

Give them the freedom they crave and help them find their own purpose within their jobs, and if their purpose lives outside of what they're doing, then help them get there. We also *must* stop expecting our managers to be all things to all people. Instead, we must look at our leadership in pairs—operational leaders who excel at maintaining must be matched with inspirational leaders who cast a vision and be more entrepreneurial.

SETTING UP YOUR MILLENNIAL TEAM MEMBERS TO EXCEL

The matrix below is something I created and use with my team members to help them chart where their current job resides and where their skills and passions lead them. This matrix helps us set up our team members to do their best work. That increases engagement and ensure our team members are empowered to lead our company toward more defining moments. Here's how it works.

The matrix maps job responsibilities across two spectrums: (1) maintaining the status quo to building for the future, and (2) from individual contributions to group, or people-focused activities. The matrix maps these out on two axes. The horizontal line, or x-axis, maps primary job responsibilities based on maintaining or building. The vertical line, or y-axis, maps primary job responsibilities based on the extent to which they are individual or people-focused.

Some activities will be building and people-focused. Others will be building and individual, maintaining and people-focused, or maintaining and individual contributions. To find out where each team member's current responsibilities fall, print a blank matrix, and put dots on the matrix based on their primary duties and day-to-day responsibilities.

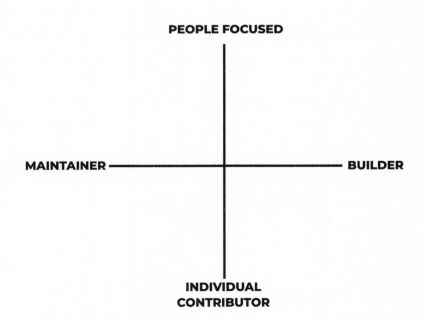

After filling out the matrix, you may discover some employees whose duties and responsibilities fit perfectly for their skills, dreams, and passions. You may also find people performing duties that are not a good fit for their skills, dreams, and passions. We found this with a team member who had been with us for three years. She's an incredible person and was very hardworking. But when we mapped out her primary job responsibilities, we discovered most of them involved maintaining through individual contributions. She was doing things such as assembling furniture and other things that only involved following directions and working alone.

We learned she was doing so well because of how talented and hardworking she was, not because she was working in an area that fit her well. All of her duties fit squarely within the bottom-left quadrant of the matrix, a copy of which I've recreated below.

Seeing this in black and white allowed us to focus on moving her closer to a role that was a better fit for where she wanted to go. In her case, we wanted to move her into a more creative role that involved more building, people-focused activities. We represented that on the matrix with a second circle and drew arrows connecting her current role to her ideal one.

We then identified several steps we could take together to help her start making the transition from maintainer/individual-contributor activities to builder/people-focused ones. We represented those steps as slash marks along the arrows. Completing those tasks would slowly transition her from her current duties to ones that would better position her to succeed.

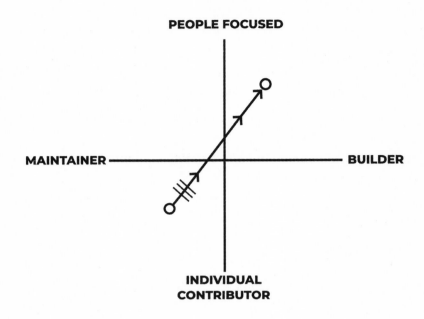

Before the matrix, she performed well but was not reaching her full potential. After the matrix, she became even more engaged and we were both working together to transition her into a role in which she would continue to excel. That helps improve her engagement and lead 22squared even closer to achieving true defining moments—especially as we help even more team members achieve similar transformations.

You can download a copy of the matrix on the Resources page at TheMillennialWhisperer.com/BookResources.

QUICK SUMMARY

- When a situation arises with a Millennial employee don't rush to disciplinary action or fire them. It's important for leaders to make the effort to understand Millennial employees' situations and show empathy toward them. Otherwise they either won't stay engaged or you'll be scrambling for their replacement.

- Millennials are a lonely generation. They also have a tendency to judge their popularity and even their self-worth by the number of "friends" and "followers" they've amassed. To build and maintain my relationships with my Millennial employees I've learned to get social with them. I follow my Millennial employees on Instagram and Facebook. I watch their stories and I make sure to hit the "like" button when they post something about their life. Following our teams on social media—not in a creepy, stalkerish way but in the same way their actual friends do—shows that we're engaged and interested in them as people. It makes them feel less lonely. I encourage those who aren't convinced that following employees on social media is a great idea to at least try it for 30 days.

- Get real with Millennial employees. They need to understand that we're human and that mistakes, rather than being grounds for discipline or dismissal, can instead be learning tools and growth opportunities.

- 70% of your job should give you energy and get you fired up but, the reality is, 30% of your job will always kind of suck. This is the 70/30 rule. Millennials should be armed with this information to avoid "the grass is always greener" complex.

MAKE IT HAPPEN.

Getting and keeping Millennials engaged is all about building quality relationships. The great news is that we can nurture these high-value relationships from many different angles. If there's any *one* point you take back to your office from this chapter, it's that creating genuine relationships is critical to getting and keeping Millennials engaged. We must learn to nurture connections with our Millennial employees consistently, transparently, and authentically.

For Boomers and Gen Xers who are used to a more stoic relationship with management, this may feel wearisome at first. But try this out for a few months, and I promise you, you'll see exponential returns on your emotional investment in your Millennial staff. Some of these leaders believe that there still needs to be a "friendship line" that is not crossed between employees and their managers, but I wholeheartedly disagree. An authentic bond and trust with employees usually ends up looking a lot like a friendship.

Here are some step-by-step actions you can take to build those relationships:

1. Follow your employees on social media and engage with their social channels.
2. Show your personal side to your employees.
3. Admit your mistakes (as early as possible).
4. Provide Millennials with an opportunity to pursue their passions within their work.
5. Encourage each employee to come up with a personal "purpose statement."
6. Focus on growing your EQ as well as your Millennial team members.

CHAPTER 4
MANAGING MILLENNIAL ANGST

Keeping Them Focused and Removing Distractions

Setting: The Snake River in Idaho; crystal-clear blue sky, lush greenery, crisp air, sparkling water.

Cast of Characters: Chris Tuff. A private fly-fishing guide.

Act 1, Scene 1

Chris: "It's a perfect day for fly-fishing!" (Thinks to himself, *Except that I don't know how to fly-fish. Whatever. How hard can it be? I'm going to get my Brad Pitt-stunt-double shot just like "A River Runs Through It." I'll post it on Instagram, and everyone will see how outdoorsy and handsome I am! I am going to make some people pretty jealous with all this cool gear."*)

Guide: "Okay, let's step in the water."

Chris: "It's freezing!"

(Chris proceeds to fumble through the water like Goofy with a bumblebee in his waders.)

Guide: "Um, how much coffee have you had? You're scaring the fish!"

Act 1, Scene 2

Chris: "Can you pretend that I caught the fish and take a photo with my iPhone?"

END

Yeah, that actually happened. I sucked at fly-fishing. The angles didn't work, the fish weren't biting, and I was miserable and muddy. So I got a fake shot for Instagram.

It was an embarrassing moment that I often share with Millennials, because I know the pressure to get that perfect shot is what they feel every single day. We need to experience moments without the filter of a phone.

And by unlocking the doors to Millennial angst, we can experience moments of much greater success. I think it's also important that I've embarrassingly admitted this story to all of my team using it as an example (remember vulnerability?).

The Pinterestation of our Generation

Millennials compare their insides to other people's outsides. You know, they scroll through social media and see only the highlights of people's lives and compare it to all the emotional, financial, and personal struggles they feel…

I am constantly reminding my employees (and myself) to stop doing this.

It's always the first day of school that you'll notice in your feeds every single Millennial parent painstakingly capturing the moment ever-so-perfectly with a blackboard cutout of their child's grade entry, favorite food, etc. Every moment needs to be perfect. Many of this generation have to send a picture to anyone in it to see if it's "good enough" to post on Instagram. Everything is perfectly curated and crafted to appear like the posts that fill their own feeds. It's *exhaaaaausting*.

It's also understandable, as Millennials grew up feeling judged by the number of likes on their class photo or followers on their Instagram account.

Millennials have everyone's highlight reels in their faces—all day, every day. This leads to massive comparison hangovers. It also inspires *some* Millennials to believe that if they could just get a different job or a different boss, with different perks, their lives would be way better.

Even more dangerous, Millennials have grown up watching a few select "unicorn" companies thrive. They've seen Mark Zuckerberg earn billions and noted the star-like ascension of Twitter, Pinterest, and Snapchat. Older Millennials saw a lot of jumping around with quick-start companies—unrealistic expectations set by sporadic successes led to dashed dreams. These older Millennials put Zuckerberg up as their poster board for success, then felt like total failures when their own entrepreneurial ideas flopped (I guess we can kind of blame Zuck for creating these behaviors, too.)

The younger Millennials at first looked like they were going to follow suit and quit as soon as new opportunities arose. But the stats are now showing us that *this* group of Millennials is craving longevity. They are seeing that they need a place where they can lean in and help shape the culture (as we discussed earlier). They want to work in an environment where they feel that they're contributing to a purpose beyond themselves and where they have opportunities for continued growth.

Yet they can get distracted by the "shiny object syndrome" of the new entrepreneurial ideas they see some of their friends pursuing.

We can manage Millennial workers' angst and fears that they're not "living the dream" of a work-from-anywhere lifestyle by *encouraging* them to pursue their side passions. If we give them even a small percentage of their day to pour energy into a side hustle, *most* of them will quickly see that building an outside business takes a lot more work than they desire to put in. Their creativity will stay engaged, but they won't leave their valuable position inside the organization to pursue a pipe dream.

The key is for Millennials to feel the freedom to explore and pursue their passions. When they know they can do this and stay within a company, they're far less likely to leave.

Our age of connectedness has helped increase Millennial angst. This generation is used to having things *now* and *fast.* Many grew up with Amazon Prime 2-day delivery; others grew up in a Snapchat world where 2-day delivery is the *slow* option. They think nothing of having groceries delivered in an hour. They see updates on their friends, enemies, and favorite celebrities in real time. They're more easily distracted than Generation Xers or Baby Boomers, and they suffer from ADHD at higher levels than older generations.

That's why they feel frustrated at the length of time it takes for them to progress within a company. As leaders, we can fix this by reframing what it looks like to move up the company ladder. We can develop checkpoints and feedback loops that continually let your Millennial team members know they're on the right track.

Throughout this chapter, I'll be bringing you specific skills and strategies to manage Millennial angst. But before I get too far down that path, let me point out how we as leaders can identify with some of the comparison struggles that keep our Millennial employees from living up to their full potential.

Nursing a Comparison Hangover

As I mentioned earlier, particular types of social media can have negative effects. As a leader of Millennials, I can confirm that these negative effects are real.

A recent University of Missouri study went so far as to link browsing Facebook and seeing photos of fancy houses, luxury cars, and expensive vacations with increased symptoms of depression.[22]

Social media can be a tool of great good, but it can also put a lot of pressure on these young people. Another study published in the *Clinical Psychological Science* journal and reported on in the New York Post noted a correlation between increased social media use and suicidal thoughts.[23] Millennials have grown up feeling measured and judged by their online presence to the extent that some of them think it would be better not to be alive. *That's heavy.*

As a result, Millennial workers can be much more *reactive* and *impulsive* than older employees. That's okay, because there are ways to manage these Millennial traits and even harness them for the good of your company—such as mindfulness training. One the flip side, it's also important to acknowledge that a lot of Millennials have an entrepreneurial bent. They've grown up in the gig economy where they can freelance or drive for Über and have a lot more control over their schedule than any of us ever did. A survey conducted by Bentley University found 66% of Millennials wanted to start their own business.[24] Knowing that's the case, there are ways we can give Millennials enough of a taste of running their own company that they'll see how great they have it in their current job.

Giving an Inch to Get a Mile

Remember that old saying, "Give them an inch, they'll take a mile?" Not true with Millennials!

Alter the statement to read, "Give them an inch, they'll give *you* a mile," and you'll be on the right track. As leaders, it is our responsibility to foster our employees' creativity yet also harness it for the good of the organization. I've said it before, but Millennials want autonomy *within* structure. They need *both*.

A perfect example of someone who's been given a large level of independence within my own company is Ansley Williams, our Senior Manager of Influencer Marketing. Remember how we discussed in the last chapter that allowing Millennials to pursue their purpose within their day jobs can help to get and keep them engaged at work?

Ansley's stated purpose is "empowering women to feel beautiful in their own skin." Rather than telling her just to find a nonprofit to volunteer with on her off hours, we made the effort to give her tasks that align with this purpose during her everyday work.

In her role at 22squared, Ansley has been able to live out her purpose by coordinating relationships between some of our key advertising clients and social media influencers. I've given her free rein to recommend the influencers she thinks will resonate most with our clients' ideal markets. And she's done a brilliant job of recommending some unexpected influencers who've helped increase our clients' revenues and ROI. Rather than give all the ad dollars to super-celebrities, Ansley has cleverly scouted *real* women who have tribes that follow their every recommendation. These influencers may not be the super-skinny, airbrushed, Insta-famous models lots of advertisers use, but their word has clout among their thousands of followers.

Allowing Ansley to *choose* which influencers we recommend to our clients honors her own purpose of peeling back the surface-level layers and showing the real women behind curated brands. Ansley wants women to know that they're valuable—no matter what they look like or what size clothes they wear—and her work here actually helps her advance that purpose. She told me, too, that it's made a big difference in her work satisfaction that she's allowed to fail. It's happened very rarely, but every one of us neglects to hit a home run every once in a while. Ansley—along with the rest of my Millennial employees—knows that I have her back.

Much like my friends who hold the "mistakes meetings," I want my Millennial employees to know that if they *do* have an idea that doesn't work the way they expected, their jobs aren't going to be in jeopardy (assuming they're giving a task their best shot). Ansley has expressed that knowing she can make a mistake without fearing for her job has allowed her to be more creative and take more risks, the vast majority of which have resulted in huge successes for 22squared.

Encouraging Your Employees' Entrepreneurial Spirit

Here are some ways—ranked from good to better to best—to nurture the Millennial entrepreneurial spirit that don't end with employees waltzing out your office doors.

Good idea:

Verbally encourage your Millennial team members when they share their entrepreneurial ideas. This strategy is totally organic and dependent on the individual leader. You're not setting aside company time or financial resources to employ this technique. You're just being human around your employees. Rather than creating an environment where they're scared to share about anything they're doing outside of work, cultivate an atmosphere where they know you'll appreciate and even encourage their outside pursuits.

You can take this a step further by offering to mentor an employee in some area where you have experience outside of working hours. For example, I've offered to teach my Millennial employees about Facebook ads if they want to quickly test whether an idea has legs in the marketplace. This lets them try out their theories and see them fail quickly, rather than risking their jobs within our company only to find out that their "brilliant new concept" was a total bust.

Better idea:

Where possible, give your Millennial team members a portion of their workday to focus on their passion or side project. *What you'll lose in productivity for that small time period, you'll gain in efficiency for the entire rest of the workday.* Remember that momentum begets momentum. When Millennials feel like they're gaining traction in one area of their life, this will carry over to the work they do within your company. How you do *anything* is how you do *everything.*

It doesn't matter so much to Millennials whether their passion projects "succeed" or "fail." *What they really care about is that they were given the opportunity to try.* When they sense that you want them to succeed—not just professionally, but personally, too—you will earn their trust. When they trust you, Millennials will go to extraordinary lengths to support your organization.

An added side benefit of encouraging Millennials to pursue their side businesses comes from the networking they'll do. While they are out and about making connections for their side companies, they'll also be painting your company in a great light. People they meet at conferences could become clients and customers of your company, too. Relationship marketing is the strongest form of currency in business today, and if you support Millennials in their outside pursuits, they'll reward you by presenting you with their contacts. Also, as I tell everyone, you'll have ups and downs and most likely when you have a side hustle it helps you overcome the downs because momentum fuels momentum, and you might just have to borrow that from your side hustle. Having raised significant capital and co-founding other startups myself, I'll go as far as helping these employees talk through capitalization tables and fundraising tips. But it's amazing how much you can find out nowadays with a $1000 Facebook ad budget whether or not an idea will be a success... many times, the ideas go unproven, and the employee decides that benefits and a consistent paycheck is the better route.

I know a lawyer whose small firm supported her side hustle. They didn't give her firm money to pursue her passions but were generous in giving her time away from the office to attend conferences and meetings as long as it was on her own dime. While she did eventually grow her side business to the point where she transitioned out of law, that firm still benefits from clients she brought in while she was out -and -about, networking and sharing her enthusiasm.

Best idea:

If you are the leader of a large organization, consider starting a business incubator program. This is a way to truly capitalize on your employees' brightest ideas. Your company can provide funding and other resources to allow your employees to pursue their most promising business goals, and then retain an ownership stake in the ideas that succeed.

Harsh and Helpful Reality

I've found that mentoring my Millennial employees in their pursuit of their side hustles actually shows them some harsh realities, which in turn helps our company retain top talent.

Entrepreneurial life is *not* for everyone; more often than not, Millennials get a small taste of it and want no more. Instead of losing your employees to their failed startups, encourage them to find a side hustle and teach them to do it. I spend ten minutes every week teaching my team about how to run a side hustle, going over everything from raising money, capitalization tables, trademarks, proformas, whatever they have questions about. And for about $2,000 and some Instagram and Facebook ads, you can quickly figure out if that side hustle has legs or not, unfortunately, most of the time it's doesn't—and that's okay. A Millennial member of our team had a great idea for a clothing company, so I helped her pursue this. After about six months, the novelty had worn off and the realities of trying to sell clothes online in such a crowded marketplace took hold, so she decided to call it quits. Now, she remains a productive member of the team.

Usually, a project is begun but burns out quickly. Nonetheless, my team's curiosity is satisfied, and their wings aren't clipped. So actually, in giving them the freedom to pursue these side hustles, we increase our retention rate of top Millennials employees. They have the freedom to see that the grass was only spray-painted green on the other side of the fence.

And on the off chance that one of your employees' side hustles *does* flourish, you will have built incredible goodwill with her by being supportive.

This book you're holding is actually my own personal example of a successful side hustle that actually helped me improve my performance within my regular role. When I first got the idea to write *The Millennial Whisperer*, I was in a period where I felt like there was more I could be doing as a manager and leader. The second that I committed to writing the book, I felt a surge of energy. It carried over into every single interaction I had inside the office, and even our clients could feel it. I'd say I became at least 50% more productive *during* the time period that I was writing the book. It's also been within this time period that my *impac*t has increased dramatically—I'll attribute that to both the side hustle and to acting upon most of the ideas in this book. I know that's at least partly due to my increased focus and drive that's carried over from my passion project.

Unplug and Unwind

One of the most progressive things that I do with the team is bringing in my friend Sarah Bristow, the founder of a health and wellness practice called Growing Grounded. She counsels the team on the importance of mindfulness and meditation, and leads the group in guided practice. Prior to each monthly session, Sarah reaches out to the team to gather ideas and current issues that they would like to address; these range from stress and anxiety to faux pas subjects such as depression. She then arranges the curriculum to meet these needs.

The most recent session talked about the importance of becoming aware of our thoughts. She guided the team to label each passing thought as one from the past, present, or future. For the visual folks, she had them place each thought in imaginary buckets with a corresponding label. Through this, the team was able to see that many of our thoughts and worries are in the past, that which we that we can't undo. Similarly, many of our worries revolve around the future events, which we can't control.

After more than a year of her group coaching, one of my Millennial employees asked, "Can we please have her in every week—this is better than getting a massage!" I quickly replied that considering I pay her directly out of my own money, I can't afford to do it weekly.

The Importance of Unplugging

Ever see that New Yorker cartoon of the guy with the cone on his head, and he says, "It keeps me from looking at my phone every two seconds?" Yeah, Millennials spend an exorbitant amount of time on their phones, and it's not just them, it's everyone. Take notice in your next meeting the amount of people who are haphazardly checking their phones throughout the meeting. We must help everyone by setting both standards and rules that help us unplug from time to time. For example, on a nice day I'll surprise the team with a status across the street outside, conjuring them to join me for a walk.

Or, I've had team meetings where everyone must put their phone at the entrance of conference room on a table where they remained stacked buzzing upon one another as we connect without distractions. I'll often times talk about my own habits openly as a way to inspire them to turn off their phones or hide them when putting their children to bed (as I try to do every night). A new mom on my team recently pulled me aside to tell me that she no longer will check email, Instagram, or anything else between the hours of 6 p.m. and 9 a.m. She said just a week into this ritual that her 8-month-old son seems to be happier and that it's added an incredible amount of anxiety relief because she can actually enjoy the moments with him.

Phone manufacturers have also taken note. allowing users to set up screen time and analytics on usage. We must unplug to unwind, and it starts with you as the leader to set that standard within your culture; everyone will benefit.

Compassion Covers a Multitude of Sins

We need to set high standards for our Millennial employees.

Then we must give them autonomy to meet those standards in the ways that feel most congruent to their own personalities and passions.

Be available for near-constant feedback. In a world that seems to be shifting more toward a "feeling" culture, feedback and criticism are sometimes seen as a faux pas, discouraged, or simply avoided. I know that for me it was something I used to never do because I was worried about hurting someone's feelings. But when I started with my new group, I decided that giving real time feedback was essential.

Not only was this effective, but people actually *craved* it. After someone presents in front of the group or to a client, I'll meet with them immediately afterward and tell them how many "ums" they said, where they lacked confidence, and what they could improve upon. But I'll also tell them everything they did well. It's like a game I play with my two daughters, "high-low-high," where I ask them to share their highlight, lowlight, and another highlight of the day. This usually unravels with highlight almost always being recess, lowlight being having to use their brains to do math and highlight being the dance party where Daddy took his shirt off while singing Right Said Fred's "I'm Too Sexy." (Yeah, this does happen often during dinners.)

Real time feedback is very similar. But guess what? I also ask *them* for their feedback on me as well. Everything should be two-way: if you're not willing to take it, then forget about dishing it out. I remember recently someone on my team took me aside, nervously, and said, "Listen, I know you don't mean to, but you use the term *you guys* a ton, and the truth is most of us are females. I just want to bring it to your attention." Atlantans tend to use y'all, but I lived in Boston until I was 13. I know I'm stubborn. Now I try to correct myself and understand that I have to walk the talk in implementing feedback.

Remember that this generation has been under a social microscope and flanked by helicopter parents their entire young lives. It may take them a bit of time to unlearn some unhealthy patterns, but they are craving real connection with inspirational leaders. When we can model for them that we truly care about their success within our organization, they will be our most loyal workers.

One of my best Millennial employees had something on his heart to share about the way we as leaders treat our employees. This guy is one of my top recruits. I'm going to keep him nameless in this story—you'll see why—but his thoughts are important to share. This employee has done phenomenal things for 22squared, but he started his career at a company he refers to as the "Lord of the Flies" office.

His manager in that office did everything wrong. She ruled by fear, pitted people against each other, and expected him to be on call 24/7.

She twisted the knife by making him work on a client pitch during his bachelor party weekend and called him on his honeymoon to berate him for approving a particular piece of social content (which she had actually also approved on his wedding day).

Here's the end of that story. This employee took all the *good* skills and training this Cruella-style boss had given him and now uses them at 22squared, where he's treated like a human being. He's given the freedom to leave work at 5 P.M. almost every day to beat the traffic (because he comes in super early to put in the hours) and is always just a text away. He's also given the freedom to discover his own purpose and passions instead of just the day-to-day of his current position. This freedom challenges him to question the status quo and to always be reaching higher and deeper within himself.

We can't rule Millennials with an iron fist. It simply doesn't work. They may suck it up and hang around for a year or so to get the experience they need. But they'll leave us to find a company whose leaders employ the skills in this book.

Train your Millennial team members and give them access to plenty of support in growing their skills in their chosen field. Whereas prior generations saw seminars and workshops as a hassle and detractor from their time dedicated to work, Millennials embrace these opportunities to expand their knowledge base.

I pay out of my own pocket for a mindfulness consultant to teach my team members how to meditate and find balance in their lives. And as I mentioned, I also dedicate time to every team member to help him or her figure out personal purpose statements, to be revealed at a Jeffersonian dinner. Millennials *do* hit what's known as quarterlife crisis because, unlike their predecessors, they are on a constant pursuit of self. So embrace the quarterlife crisis and help them on their way.

QUICK SUMMARY

- We can manage Millennials workers' angst and fears that they're not "living the dream" of a work-from-anywhere lifestyle by encouraging them to pursue their side passions.

- If we give Millennials even a small percentage of their day to pour energy into a side hustle, most of them will quickly see that building an outside business takes a lot more work than they desire to put in. Their creativity will stay engaged, but they won't leave their valuable position inside the organization to pursue a pipe dream.

- The key is for Millennials to feel the freedom to explore and pursue their passions. When they know they can do this and stay within a company, they're far less likely to leave.

- Verbally encourage your Millennial team members when they share their entrepreneurial ideas.

- Rather than creating an environment where they're scared about anything they doing outside of work, cultivate an atmosphere where they know you'll appreciate and even encourage their outside pursuits.

- Give your Millennial team members a portion of their workday to focus on their passion or side project. The best way to encourage them is, if you are the leader of a large organization, to consider starting a business incubator program.

MAKE IT HAPPEN.

One could argue that Millennials have it harder than any generation before them. Yet they remain so hopeful and open to possibilities that you risk losing them to a "grass is greener" start-up or their own entrepreneurial vision if you don't manage them wisely.

Follow these specific steps to manage Millennial angst and make the most of Millennial talent within your organization.

1. Learn to rein in your Millennial team members without stifling their drive and entrepreneurial spirit.

2. Give them a safe space to fly. Allow them to use a small portion of their workday to explore passion projects.

3. If you have the funds and capacity, consider beginning a business incubator program to keep you Millennial employees' "side hustles" in-house.

4. Foster an environment where your Millennial team members know that you'll have their back if they do make a mistake.

5. Show some compassion. This generation faces challenges that you and I never had to deal with. Empathy goes a long way with people who are used to judgment.

6. Teach your Millennial team members tools such as mindfulness to help them manage their stresses.

CHAPTER 5

REWARDING AND RECOGNIZING MILLENNIALS

Saving Money and Finding
Better Incentives

Cock-a-doodle-do—or don't? Would you want to work next to a blue, 10-foot aluminum rooster for a month?

You would, if you were an employee at Domo, a Utah cloud-based software company. Back in the day, when employees (called Domosapiens) first began here, managers asked sales employees to add their favorite song to the company's music playlist. Then, at the beginning of each week, when the top sales rep was announced, lights flashed, an air horn sounded, and their favorite song blared over the loudspeaker. The large blue rooster was rolled out to sit beside the employee's desk as a symbol of sales prowess.

It's almost too crazy to believe, but this is exactly the type of creative reward that keeps Millennials jockeying for the top position.

Millennials don't see "success" the same way that Boomers and Gen Xers do. For us, it was all about hard work and cash rewards. We wanted to make it to the top and be paid handsomely for our work. We were all about the grind and the hustle.

If a manager had told me I was getting a promotion without a pay raise, I would've started looking for a new position. Boomers especially were taught to make as much money as possible so they could retire early and finally start to enjoy life.

The Why Wait Generation

Millennials aren't waiting for retirement to begin living out their dreams. In fact, they'd revolt against that idea. Many of them saw their parents bust it their entire lives only to have their retirement funds obliterated with the 2008 crash.

Chances are that your Millennial team members aren't responding to traditional rewards and recognition systems. They don't measure their worth in terms of houses, cars, and bank accounts (like a lot of us did). Millennials only care about those things only to the extent that they need them to survive. They'd choose a smaller apartment so they can have a bigger travel budget. (One study by Hilton found that 53% of Millennials love to travel for business, and 53% will also create reasons for travel so they can get on the road—conference in Portland, anyone?) They'll forgo the fancy car to have a month-long sabbatical. They're all about *experiences* over *material things*.

Millennials view success as more *qualitative* than *quantitative*. They've noted that their passions evolve and that people evolve. They desire to see that change and growth reflected in the positions they hold at work.

Millennials aren't very concerned about a straight path to growth. They want growth on *their* terms. They want recognition and rewards in a way that feels fully supportive to their psyche. And as I tell everyone,

"If you're going to bed at night and not completely and utterly exhausted from propping up your Millennial team members, then you haven't done it enough today." It's hard to retain Millennials, show studies alongside workforce experiences. The Deloitte Millennial 2016 Survey found that most Millennials—68% of them—didn't plan to stay with an employer longer than three years. Slightly less than half of Millennials surveyed—44%—didn't plan on staying longer than two years. More than a fifth—22%—hoped to leave their employer within the next year. This isn't surprising. After all, leaders and their companies have been operating one way for decades. That way doesn't naturally build the levels of trust and transparency we know Millennials crave. But if we innovate how we lead, given what we know about Millennials in the workforce, we can become outliers with a much higher retention rate.

For example, a Forbes article from 2017 highlighted an online cloud-based accounting company called Freshbooks and told the story of their Manager of Support Operations, Grace Antonio, who built a team of 86% Millennials with a 93% retention rate. So how did Grace build such a loyal team out of Millennials? For one, she used hiring strategies. In the interview process, Grace identified qualities that her "retainable" employees had in common and figured out whether or not these qualities were shared in a prospective employee. By being particular about hiring, Grace was able to build a team whose traits coincided with the retainable qualities she was looking for. It's just another example of how strategies such as "doing the dance" can help you hire Millennial employees with staying power.

Grace also made the company a customer-centric culture rather than a company-centric culture. She makes all new hires at Freshbooks do a month of customer support. This leaves her employees with the understanding that they are helping people in the real world rather than just raking in the dollars for a faceless corporation.

The results are higher engagement and increased loyalty. The stats further echo what we touched on earlier in the book: Millennial employees want to feel like their work is purposeful. A whopping 74% of job seekers are searching for a job where they feel like their work really matters. Those who feel like they're doing a meaningful job are three times more likely to stay.

Anytime I get frustrated with the perceived lack of loyalty among Millennials, I remind myself that it totally makes sense that they'd be nervous to spend 20 or 30 years with a company after they witnessed what happened to their parents after the recession. And that study that found 75% of employees under the age of 34 think job-hopping would benefit their careers. I use findings that like that to fuel creative ideas for recognizing and rewarding my Millennial employees so they'll never want to leave.

MOTIVATING OUR MILLENNIAL WORKERS

Meredith Guerriero, who has worked at Google and Facebook and is now the US Head of Partnerships at Pinterest, asks each potential hire one key question: *"What motivates you?"* This question has helped Meredith become an empowering leader and get top performance from her Millennial employees. She emphasizes that Millennials really need a one-to-one management style, clear expectations, and transparency from the top down to do their best work. She makes a point of letting her recruits in on company KPIs before setting BHAGS (Big Hairy Audacious Goals) that everyone is excited to work toward. Meredith says that she gets the best performance from Millennial employees when she gives them feedback in the moment. Real time feedback is a tool for building trust and transparency.

We have about a 12-hour window to reward and recognize our teams for a task well done before the praise feels stale. Millennials grew up with instant gratification. They didn't have to wait in line to buy the new hit album. They just pushed a button, and it was on their phone instantaneously. They post a photo on Instagram and check back in one minute to find 50 new likes. We must hero our people up in real time, ideally while the endorphins from their achievement are still pumping. Just as you are now drawing on your Millennial team members to craft pieces of the company culture, make sure to tailor each employee's promotion plan to his or her desired outcomes. Asking a question like "What motivates you?" or "What's one big goal you want to achieve?" will help you give rewards that your Millennial team members will work hard to earn.

Remember Dr. Peter Boulden, the dentist? He has a unique way of rewarding his Millennial employees: he lets them reward *each othe*r. He's got a program called "ADS (Atlanta Dental Spa) Bucks." Every month, each employee is given a $50 check, and the only catch is that the employee has to give it to another team member who supported him or her the most that month. Team members go above and beyond for each other because they know that lending a helping hand may also get them multiple $50 checks. It's also helped Dr. Boulden as he reviews staff. If someone comes to him asking for a raise, there's a clear record of how many ADS Bucks that employee has been given. The whole team speaks to identify the standout employees.

Dr. Boulden's ADS Bucks program is something that really helps in the age of Instagram where getting a "like" or comment on a social media post is a dopamine hit to people. ADS Bucks are real-world, tangible "likes" that team members can earn to get the recognition they crave in front of their colleagues (plus a few extra dollars in their pocket). Dr. Boulden describes it as "a form of social proofing in public, amongst our team."

Another benefit is the social proof and dopamine are tied to behavior that helps the company become a better, more profitable place to work. One of the best parts about the ADS Bucks program is how tied it is to adding value to the team and the company as a whole. "It reinforces a team-based meritocracy, rewarding people who bring the most value to the rest of the team," Dr. Boulden says. "I consider people who get piles of ADS Bucks each month, our 'value monsters.' And if someone doesn't get ADS Bucks very often, maybe it's time for a self-audit to see how you can help your colleagues in such a way that gets noticed (and recognized) when it comes time to distribute the ADS Bucks."

Saving Face

Rewarding Millennial employees can be as simple—and as low-cost—as making the time to meet with them face-to-face. When you make the effort to sit and talk with them for 10 minutes out of your workday, you are cultivating the type of genuine relationship we discussed earlier. You are showing Millennials that they are valuable within your organization, and that's going to inspire them to work harder for you. Holding one-on-ones with our Millennials can be one of our best investments into our teams.

Michael Hibbison, a VP in merchandising at The Home Depot, swears by the two ways in which he connects with his team members on an individual basis—bi-weekly meetings and monthly one-on-one lunches. "Our weekly touch-bases are an essential part of our business," says Hibbison. "I give the respective team member the option to choose what we talk about, work or personal. I don't bring an agenda, and leave it completely up to them. Some choose to talk about work. Others mix it up. One employee has been meeting with me for more than a year and has only brought up work *twice*. She prefers we spend our time getting to know each other on a human level."

Setting aside this time to give each team member genuine, uninterrupted attention and the freedom to talk about whatever is most important to *team members* has helped Home Depot form bonds that are much stronger than what many people typically expect from colleagues. "The lunches are much of the same," says Hibbison. "We try to go off-site to a more casual setting where we won't run into people we know who may interrupt our discussions." These bi-weekly touch-base meetings and monthly lunches are a perfect example of relationship building and developing deeper perspectives about the company, its purpose, and its place in society. Hibbison adds that The Home Depot also experiences regular informal meetings, and that the number of times a day associates "pop in" to discuss things is incredible. This makes the touch-bases and lunches more personal. "Leaders must be open to fewer scheduled meetings as Millennials don't have a problem just popping in for discussion," he says. "A leader must have a true open-door (if there is a door at all) policy allowing for these 5- to 10-minute discussions. Given the speed at which we are working, we shouldn't always wait for a formal meeting to make decisions or bounce ideas off each other. Millennials want to feel like they are equals, and not another rung down on the org chart."

We give a lot of face time and a lot of company recognition at 22squared. For example, we hold regular in-person meetings. These are touch points where are employees get to see that we're in the trenches with them. We start out each meeting with our "22 snaps" tradition I mentioned earlier.

1. We recognize our team's great achievements in front of their colleagues.
2. We're reminded to keep looking for the things our team members do well.

We also give many different layers of rewards at 22squared. We have agency-wide recognition programs, department-level rewards, and even peer-to-peer awards. We've also learned that a lot of our Millennial employees crave shout-outs and novel experiences more than they crave the traditional cash bonuses. For example, if I have a Millennial employee who's gone above and beyond, I could give him a $5,000 bonus check. Or I could give him $2,000 in $100 bills, presented to him in front of all his office mates, and then have an armed guard walk him to the bank to deposit it (this is actually what my friend Doug Busk told me as the more extreme examples of creative compensation and rewards). Which option will make the bigger impression? When I'm choosing a reward for my employee, I'm also looking at my employee's personality to see if it's someone who craves attention or someone who prefers to fly under the radar.

Finding Out What Motivates Each of Your Employees and Creating Unique Experiences

Recognizing employees is another area in which Chandler McCormack and OxBlue focuses a lot of time and attention. McCormack considers recognizing employees an "art with some overlap" with creating unique but simple employee experiences.

"I can't emphasize enough how diverse people are when it comes to recognition," he explained. "My managers understand this truth. If a manager came to me asking to recognize her team using mostly money, chances are they'd either be being lazy managers, projecting their own feelings onto others, or are not in touch with their own emotional needs or the needs of their team members," he continued.

To better understand how his team members preferred to be recognized, he sent his team of nearly 100 employees a survey asking them about how they preferred to be recognized. To his surprise, his team listed more than a dozen options, including cash, public recognition, additional company opportunities, and even handwritten notes.

One of the more impactful strategies OxBlue has used to recognize employees is through creating unique experiences for team members. For example, McCormack surprised a group of eight Millennials from different departments on a Porsche Driving Experience. He didn't tell them where they were going, but when they got there, each team member got to race demo laps and enjoy a great lunch together.

McCormack has done this before, too, planning a trip for team members who hit a goal and only telling them to meet at the airport, creating special games he and his team members play, and even giving thoughtful gifts to his employees in addition to their cash bonuses. Experiences and thoughtful gifts go a long way, he explained to me, adding "If it's just money, people quickly forget about it."

McCormack encourages his leaders to identify unique ways to recognize their team members. He's passionate about how impactful individualized recognition and unique experiences can be on our companies, so passionate he shared several additional tips, strategies, and warnings on an exclusive video interview I've posted for you to watch (for free) on the Resources page at TheMillennialWhisperer.com/BookResources.

Bringing in Outside Resources

Every two months, I help organize something called our "creator series" where we bring in people from outside the agency to help our employees think about creative and change a bit differently. We gather all of our employees and bring in outside creators to help our employees see things through new eyes. We've had everyone from comic Gilbert Gottfried to TV personality Dolvett Quince. You'd be surprised how these fireside chats help get everyone excited about what we're building.

(Might I add that we *do not* pay our speakers, either—many just want to speak to a large audience and share their thoughts.)

It's also incredibly worthwhile to look inside your own company, to another department, for inspiration. Companies spend countless dollars and resources sending their employees to conferences. I tell my crew that they're not going to South By Southwest (SXSW, a go-to for digital ad agencies) to party for four days. Instead, they should be living every day like it's SXSW, learning from our own top tech talent in addition to outside speakers. For example, in our manager training series, I'll come and give a talk about how to establish a culture within a culture. There are so many experts under your own roof who will add value and garner great experience presenting to other parts of the organization.

Grown-Up Participation Trophies

I know, I know. I promised no participation trophies. And I meant it. But we can still learn from and adapt the "participation trophy principle" to help motivate our Millennials in a way that's focused on production and profits. That's where this comes in.

Millennials love praise. They grew up with a constant stream of adoration and attention. So, if your Millennial staffer has done something well and you want that achievement repeated and multiplied, make sure to highlight her accomplishment. Don't save your "attaboys" and pats on the back for the big wins; celebrate the small successes along the way.

Also, when giving praise, we must **make it authentic**. Eye contact, genuine smiles, and specific compliments will garner much more success than the same tired old catchphrase. We need to let them know *why* we appreciate their effort. "Thanks for that research. It really helped me on the sales call" is much better than just a plain "Thanks for the research." This generation of workers grew up getting participation trophies and accolades just for showing up. I know it's annoying, but we (and the generations above us) created that system. There are ways to use that to our advantage now, though, and the best thing is that some of the recognition Millennials crave doesn't cost a penny.

An example of free rewards is the GIF-off I mentioned earlier. For example, when someone does something awesome in my department at 22squared, I send around an email congratulating them and beginning a department-wide GIF-off. I send the email to one person, who adds a creative GIF and sends it to someone new, and so on, and so on. Our Millennials love this recognition, and it's become a real team-building exercise. And you know what—it's authentic and awesome. You can either build your people or tear them down. You can either rule with a carrot or rule with a stick. **The carrot wins every time**.

The decision-makers at a company must see the Millennials doing something great. One of my Millennial team members led a killer presentation. She owned the whole room. Three hours after the meeting, I sent her an email, copying our CEO and CFO and telling her how blown away I was by her presentation. Even something simple can make a big impact. We give out these commemorative tokens when someone does something excellent in our department. They cost about $58, and they're seen as a status symbol. Giving out that token doesn't cost us much at all, but it builds a lot of goodwill among our employees.

A friend of mine, a former lawyer, mentioned that in the law environment, what Millennials really want—more than a bonus check—is their names on the legal briefs. And the order of names on the brief matters, too. This generation wants to be seen and acknowledged for their contributions. It's worth making the effort to find creative ways to honor the high performers, because there's almost always an accompanying performance boost when a Millennial is recognized in a way that resonates.

A New View on Reviews

Several years ago, I was visiting San Francisco on a business trip to Facebook headquarters, and Über had just launched. I was so excited when I opened the app at the airport for the first time and I could see the black SUV coming to pick me up. The driver (we'll call him Scott) was amazing and very courteous (a huge upgrade from the yellow cabs of SF). When he dropped me off, Scott said, "Don't forget to give me a review!" The app gave me the option of 5 stars, but I had no idea what they indicated, so I gave him 3 solid stars. Four hours later when I finished my meetings at Facebook headquarters, I called for an Über— and there was Scott coming back. When he opened the door to his black SUV, he was fuming at me, yelling, "THREE stars? You're going to get me kicked out!" I quickly apologized and told him I thought three stars was a really good score. I learned to only give five stars unless there was an issue with my Über.

Years later, I realized that I could use my confusion to clarify our own review system at 22squared, one that now helps reward (or reprimand) Millennials in a very helpful way. Now, we've moved our reviews to a grade system. Our employees receive an A, B, C, or Needs Improvement. We also added a way to give qualitative data along with these scores with feedback on they could improve. Most of the discussion, though, is around their strengths.

Tangible reviews provide tangible results. Robby Kukler, the owner of Fifth Group Restaurants in Atlanta (I'll share more of his story later) has set up a very accountable system for management teams: bonus plans related to restaurant performance. (All managers at Fifth Group are on bonus plans, important to remember as we recognize and reward Millennial contributions.) It comes down to three key points of sales, profitability (Robby shares the financials and certain earnings numbers with employees) and guest awareness. The last point really sets Fifth Group apart. The company has created a formula that includes a "net promoter" score (how likely guests are willing to recommend a restaurant to friends); an online, social media guest sentiment score; a "white glove inspection" score, and secret diners from inside the company who rate their experience. Fifth Group shares all of this information, good and bad, with the entire company for both praise and development.

What if we could all have such awareness of our own companies? We can—by including Millennials in our performance analyses.

Purposeful Praise

Another great way to reward and recognize your Millennial team members is to connect *your* praise with *their* stated purpose. For example, you could give a top team member a whole day of paid vacation to work on their passion project. I'm pretty open with my team about staying connected with their purpose. I try to build in ways for them to marry purpose with their "official" job duties as part of our team. I even tell them that if they're feeling like they're dreading coming in to work for two days in a row—and it's not because of their own procrastination— they need to look at getting a new gig.

Find ways to keep a pulse on what will really drive your Millennial team members to produce results in your company. We do this exercise where I have an employee write down on the left side of a piece of paper everything that fires her up, and on the right side of the paper, everything that zaps her energy. Then I make decisions on which tasks I assign based on that feedback. I've created a purpose template you can use with your own team. Just head on over to the research page at TheMillennialWhisperer.com/BookResources. You can download it and adapt it to your needs. I would love to hear your feedback on how this exercise works for you; it's been super successful for our team.

QUICK SUMMARY

- Millennials are all about experiences more than material things. They don't measure their worth in terms of houses, cars, and bank accounts (like a lot of us did). They'd choose a smaller apartment so they can have a bigger travel budget. They'll forgo the fancy car to have a month-long sabbatical. Millennials are more qualitative than quantitative.

- Real-time feedback is a good way to build trust and transparency. We have about a 12-hour window to reward and recognize our teams for a task well done before the praise feels stale. We must hero our people up in real time, ideally while the endorphins from their achievement are still pumping.

- You can either build your people or tear them down. You can either rule with a carrot or with a stick. The carrot wins every time.

—— MAKE IT HAPPEN. ——

Here are some concrete recognitions and reward systems you can put in place to help them feel acknowledged and appreciated.

1. Allow each of your Millennial team members to chart a success course within your company that fosters the best in his or her personal and professional development.

2. Progress within your organization should not follow a straight path for every employee. Customize career paths for what your Millennial team members long to accomplish.

3. Make sure that you spend as much time *within* your organization as you do outside of it.

4. Rewarding Millennials is insufficient. You must also *recognize* them. Here are easy ways to recognize Millennials and keep them bringing their best efforts to work:

   a. Say, "Thank you." Say it publicly. One way is to CC the department head or division leader when you send a thank-you email to a Millennial for something great they did.

   b. Celebrate every work anniversary. Make a big deal about each year someone spends working within your organization. Millennials have a lot of options. They're choosing you, so honor them for that decision.

   c. Get creative with the way you recognize Millennials. Make the rewards you hand out something that your Millennial team members will swoon over. For example, your employee might jump up and down over front-row seats to her favorite musician's concert even though that costs much less than the $2,000 bonus you originally planned on giving her.

   d. Allow your Millennial team members to choose who gets recognized. Similar to how Dr. Boulden lets his employees choose who gets their $50 monthly bonus, you can implement a system where your Millennial team members recognize each other's efforts via systems you put in place.

   e. Research your employees' special interests to provide them with the most meaningful rewards. In many cases, an extra week off might mean more to a Millennial than an additional check would.

   f. Gamify your recognition and rewards processes. Millennials grew up with games and apps on their mobile devices, and they resonate with the systematized achievements that come along with these games.

Reward and recognize *everything* your Millennial employees do that you desire more of.

Recognize your team's accomplishments *in real time.*

If you're feeling totally spent from recognizing and rewarding your people at the end of each day, that's when you know you're doing it right! I'm kidding, but only a little. Your team is your greatest asset. Their innovation and energy—when combined with long-term loyalty—can earn your company more money and prestige than *any* marketing strategy or customer service initiative. You have to protect this most important asset and guard it with your life. That includes forging real relationships with your team members, extolling achievements, and doing everything in your power to let them know how valuable they are.

Find your own Millennial Whisperer. Let's just pause here and acknowledge that you may be feeling overwhelmed and out of your element as you implement a new Millennial-friendly rewards-and-recognition protocol within your organization. If that's the case, I've got you covered. I've taken all my top skills and strategies for getting the most out of Millennials and trained a select group of certified Millennial Whisperers who are available to consult within your organization. Visit the Resources page at TheMillennialWhisperer.com/BookResources to learn more and check on their availability.

CHAPTER 6

GETTING THE MOST OUT OF MILLENNIALS

Unleashing the Full Power of the Your Team

One of my favorite expressions is, "If you've never thrown an axe badly, you've never really lived."

Okay, so I made that one up. But it's true—as my team and I discovered at Bad Axe Throwing Atlanta, where I paid for three hours of hurling dangerously sharp tools against wooden targets. It was an experience that allowed us to blow off steam and find increased energy for work, because more than any other generation, Millennials are obsessed with experiences. Our productivity was up at least 50 percent for the week after Bad Axe Throwing.

The Next Steps

We've walked pretty far together down the path of maximizing your Millennial team members' performance. By now, we have everything we need to build a company culture that attracts the right Millennial employees. We have strategies to motivate those Millennials in a way that really resonates with them and doesn't drain your budget. And we have strategies to help each team member get their work aligned with his or her passions. We're communicating with our Millennial team transparently and giving them plenty of autonomy within a clearly designated structure. And we're leading with inspiration and regularly recognizing and rewarding our teams.

But there are still a few additional strategies we have at our disposal to really get our Millennials motivated and producing. These things have made a big difference in getting the most out of my Millennial team, and I'm excited to share them with you, too.

22 Acts

I spend a lot of time thinking of creative ways to keep my team engaged and build morale. Some of them work well. Others don't. It's not always easy, especially on those occasions where a big deal doesn't go our way. But like the Unified team turns mistakes to motivation and learning, I've realized the times things don't go our way are the exact times I've experienced the most impact from showing appreciation for my team. And the best part is these ideas are coming from all our departments (not just HR).

One of these times involved what we call "22 Days of 22 Acts" which was the idea of one of our top creative talents, Mindy Adams. Yeah, we do a lot of things in groups of 22. With 22 Days of 22 Acts, we handed out an abundant supply of Post-It notes to each employee and encouraged them to write each other notes of appreciation.

We then dedicated a wall to the project and asked our team to post the notes on the wall so the entire department could be encouraged by the positive actions their teammates were taking.

Cost: Maybe $15

Impact: Huge. It ended up being a huge display of camaraderie that people still talk about. (For more examples of low-cost perks that have a big impact, visit TheMillennialWhisperer.com/BookResources.)

Here are three photos of the wall with everyone's accolades displayed:

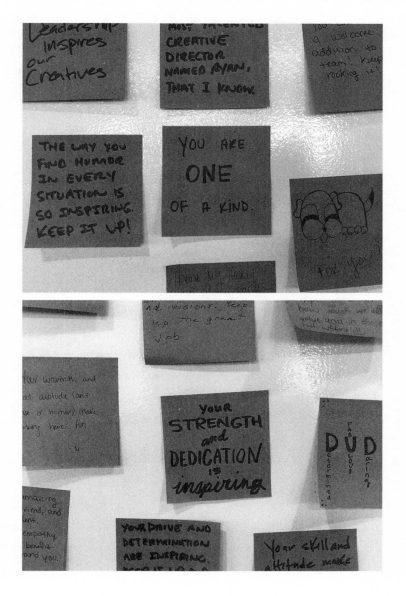

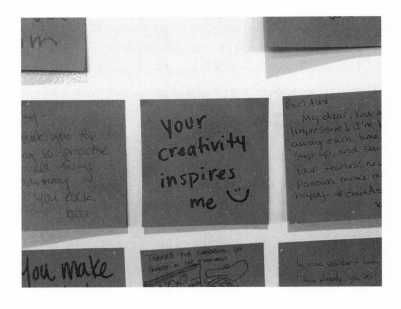

"When 22 Acts happened, I was in the middle of one of my darkest times, and I received countless notes that somehow managed to highlight and celebrate the things I'm most self-conscious about. It sparked something within me professionally, yes, but also personally: I committed to my mental health so that I'd be a better teammate, mentor, and manager—the person so many of my colleagues thought I was."

—Meg Roberts, VP, Content Marketing Director, 22squared

How many stories do you hear of simple, inexpensive initiatives having such a profound impact on employees? As a side note, as soon as Meg heard I was writing this book, she offered to share more of her story—an amazing tribute to the power of positivity.

The Transformation in the Transaction

Figuring out how to get the most from my Millennial employees has been a process, and there are a few things I've had to really feel into. I now look at my team as my biggest investment. These are the people who—if they aren't already leaders within the company—will become the next generation of managers and department heads. I've had to shift my own thinking to have a long-term perspective of how I can pour into my team now in a way that will yield future dividends.

Investing in your employees is a great way to build their loyalty and willingness to go the extra mile for you. Putting money into tools and training that equip your Millennial team members to do their jobs better can absolutely transform their job performance and company-wide profitability. Companies that invested in their employees earned themselves top spots on the 2014 *Fortune 100 Best Companies to Work For.* They didn't just land a top spot for investing in their employees; their revenues increased by an average of 22.2% and they added new employees at a rate that was five times higher than the national average.

Many leaders *aren't* doing a great job in getting the most out of their team, so it's really an opportunity for those of us who are willing to adapt to set ourselves apart. I saw a study conducted by Sirota Consulting where they followed 2.5 million employees in 237 private, public, and not-for-profit organizations in 89 countries around the world for a period of 10 years. They found that only 51% of workers were satisfied with the recognition they received after a job well done. A survey conducted by Gallup in 2016 found that only one in three US workers agreed that they had received recognition or praise for doing good work in the past seven days. I know that anyone reading this book can get better team feedback than that!

Recognizing your employees is important because it makes them happier. And happiness in employees increases their potential, loyalty, and productivity. I found a study that showed happy employees are, on average, 12% more productive than their less-happy counterparts. Another big bonus to showing appreciation for your employees is that you grow their trust levels. Nearly 90% of employees who received thanks or recognition from their boss indicated higher levels of trust in that boss. On the other hand, of those employees who didn't receive thanks or recognition from their boss, only 48% indicated they trusted their higher-ups. And a final benefit of recognizing your employees' accomplishments is that they'll feel more respected. If you'd like to keep your top talent around longer, then it's pivotal that you make them feel respected. The stats don't lie, and according to US Bureau of Labor Statistics, the vast majority of employees who decided to switch to a different career said that the reason why they left was because they felt a lack of respect.

Next-Level Productivity

Taking some simple actions that might appear to result in your employees having fewer hours clocked can actually make them far more productive. Encouraging team bonding has resulted in some huge wins at 22squared, and my colleagues in other industries have reported similar outcomes when they've tried such activities. Workplace relationships (platonic ones, of course) generally increase employee engagement. *Gallup Management Journal* surveyed 1,003 employees nationwide. Respondents were questioned about their relationships at work. The research showed that engaged employees are much more likely than others to say that their organization encourages close friendships at work. Fifty-one percent of employees who strongly agree that their organization encourages close friendships at work also report being "extremely satisfied" with their place of employment.

I've mentioned mindfulness training. It's no secret that mindful employees are healthier and more focused. General Mills, Ford, Google, Target, Adobe, Goldman Sachs, Davos . . . all of these mega-productive companies incorporate mindfulness exercises into their workday. One company, Aetna, estimates that since instituting its mindfulness program, it has saved about $2,000 per employee in healthcare costs and gained about $3,000 per employee in productivity. Seeing stats like that inspired me to bring a mindfulness instructor into our department each month, and I can vouch that the positive effects have been worth the minimal cost.

Answering "Let's" with "By when?"

Years ago, I was at Facebook headquarters with my buddy Geoff Clawson (who now runs the apparel company Birdwell Beach Britches). We were talking about all of the changes happening in the digital landscape and I told him, "Let's move some of our budgets around and really push hard with Facebook." I looked over at him as I was overcome with excitement (passion disorder taking over), and he answered me with "By when?" I then answered with a date.

Geoff instantly made me accountable to an idea or action with one simple question. This technique was one of the influences and pieces of training that Sheryl Sandberg brought to the company as COO and the results were incredibly impactful. All of us, no matter the generation or how highly aspirational we are, oftentimes fail to follow through with ideas, meetings, and commitments. By training our Millennial workforce to answer their "Let's" with a "By when?" we bring instant accountability.

"We should grab lunch or coffee soon . . ."

"By when?"

See, it works.

Feast of Fools?

If there's any industry that—pardon the pun—caters to stereotypes about Millennials, it's the restaurant industry. Take it from Robby

Kukler, a Founding Partner of the Fifth Group Restaurants, which has more than 900 employees in Atlanta and generates nearly $50 million in annual revenue. Among this generation of instant gratification and constant distractions, a scene might play out like this:

"I can't come in to work at El Taco today because I have tickets to Jason Mraz."

(Pause) "Well, if you don't show up today, you know you won't have a job."

(Minor pause) "Okay."

Or like this: "I'm on my way to Chicago and won't be coming back." Millennials might be challenged by long commutes into the city, or parking, or caring for elderly parents. Why work in the fickle restaurant market when they could drive Über or, say, do freelance design?

Why indeed? Kukler's ingredients for attracting and retaining Millennials—a culture that is equal parts people, community, and environment—create a job that is more than just a place to work, which is a recipe for success.

Kukler calls his restaurants "the ultimate team sport." If you're a server, then you're the left guard, and don't worry about the quarterback (cook). If we all do our job well, the whole team wins. We all make a team. Also, at the beginning of every school year, every hourly employee receives a backpack filled with supplies for each of their children in grades K through 12—names inscribed and all. Fifth Group restaurants compost and recycle religiously, have banned straws, and serve 90% of beer and water in cans or from the tap to reduce their environmental footprint. Restaurant managers also exercise empathy by often taking care of parking or meals for workers who commute and are let off early if business is slow.

Team training and onboarding at Fifth Group revolves around the company's purpose and values, which drives home that it is a family taking care of one another to therefore better take care of its guests.

Fifth Group also exercises a key point in retaining Millennials: promote from within. Employees have risen from support servers to managers, chefs, and beyond, learning all aspects of the business from the moment they first clock in. Future restaurateur? Yes, please! It's a learning organization, and people want to work at a Fifth Group restaurant—instead of avoiding showing up when any opportunity for distraction arises—because of this strong ethos.

"Miserable people don't create good delicious food or go out of their way to exceed their guests' expectations," says Kukler.

Taste more tips from the highly successful, Millennial-driven Fifth Group at TheMillennialWhisperer.com/BookResources

Cut Your Millennial Team Members Some Slack: Flex Work Schedules

We talk about work-life balance, yet in reality, it's much more like work-life integration. Millennials *must* be trusted to get their work done, to tally their own vacation (if a vacation policy still exists), and determine when to come to work in the morning. The mobile phone has changed *everything*. Expectations oftentimes include 24/7 responses, and it's nearly impossible to find balance nowadays (emails, IM, and text messages—it never stops).

If an employee can't be trusted to get the work done, then they don't deserve to be on your team. If someone wants to work from home for a change of scenery, I let them work from home, and you know what? The work product from home is often just as good as that from the office. As a service industry, we need to be there for our clients, and it's essential we work around our hive (office), but that doesn't mean that working people can't do it. The last thing people in salaried positions want to feel is that they're punching a time card.

For new moms, this struggle is even more real. The first thing I tell every new mom prior to their return is, "You can come and go as you please, and if anyone questions that, you can send them to me—you come in when you want and leave when you want." And you know what? This works! I believe some organizations struggle with this because managers think, "They need to pay their dues the same way I had to when I was juggling a new family." The truth is **times are different.** Expectations are different, and these employees need to have some slack cut for them. Take, for example, our employee Alok Nath, who's been with us for 10 months. When I asked how 22squared was different than his previous employer, he said, "When my daughter Meera has a big soccer game, I know that the company supports my decision to be at the game and *not* at work." It's with this that the application of work-life integration takes form.

Still, flex time is a sensitive subject. Even Facebook (renowned for its generous maternity and paternity leave and bountiful benefits) struggles with this. In *Wired,* Eliza Khuner writes about resigning from Facebook after feeling frustrated with its family policies—and receiving more than 5,500 reactions of support.[25]

Flex work is a give-and-take relationship. If employees take undue advantage of it, managers must react right away so as to not ruin it for everyone else. Also, remember "protect this house" from Chapter 1? We must create a system where people cover for one another and hold one another accountable. I think you'd be surprised at how effective this can be.

Ben Kirshner of Elite SEM lives by this . . . he also sets an example by working from home outside of Philadelphia. Instead of driving for two hours, he'll take calls and video conferences from his home office many Fridays.

This is also an opportunity to build trust. As Meg Roberts at 22squared says of flex time: "When someone feels like they are taking advantage of the freedom, there needs to be an open dialogue about it. Because managers (even Millennial ones!) don't want to be taken advantage of by their team members."

Slow Down to Speed Up

One of the best things we've done to get the most out of our Millennial team at 22squared is help them slow down. So many people think that multitasking increases productivity, but it actually hinders it.

Millennials grew up with so many distractions, and they tend to bring some to the office—such as social media notifications, personal emails, and texts.

As leaders, we can model this "slow down to speed up" principle for our teams. Raj Choudhury, the president of Brightwave, blocks off 50% of his time to interact personally with his team. He's an example of a leader who's figured out that his time is best spent face-to-face with his top talent, rather than trying to do a hundred different less-important tasks. He's created the bandwidth in his schedule to keep constant communication with his team, and as a result, they give him their all.

I've tried to model a similar strategy at 22squared. When I'm in the office, I have a rule that I don't call or email someone if I can walk to their desk instead. As a result, I log about three miles a day—a bonus result is that I need less gym time! Because I make the effort to walk around and interact with my team, they've learned to have in-person conversations with other team members instead of just messaging them. This has helped us eliminate our Millennial employees' tendency to sit on their phones all day (which used to lead to a lot of lost time, because once they pick up that phone, they're doing personal stuff in addition to our work).

Emphasizing the importance of in-person meetings is essential since instinct will lead Millennials to talk in person rather than to just text, email, or IM. This better attitude and instinct will lead Millennials to be effective leaders because so much of life happens from one person to another. I encourage everyone to follow suit by getting out of their seats and walking over to the desks of their team members and to *go see* clients.

Serial entrepreneur Dave Williams recently founded a start-up in Lisbon, Portugal. "My story is based on starting a business in a foreign country with two young Millennial business partners," he says. "When they first arrived, we didn't have any customers as they were just cold calling from their bedroom with little success. I told them to do the opposite and to get out of the apartment, go to where the customers hang out—co-work spaces, coffee shops, meetup events . . . Within a week, we had several customers and industry connections, and the business was off the ground. The point is don't get stuck messaging, calling, and sitting behind the screen. Get out there and shake hands to build your brand."

Sweet Swag

We can also encourage our Millennial employees to go the extra mile by building in regular rewards that they'll actually love using. These don't have to be expensive—in fact, it's often better if they're not.

For example, just like we do "22 snaps" at the beginning of each meeting to recognize the great things our team members have accomplished, we also give "22 claps" to recognize employees who get peer-to-peer awards. The whole department claps 22 times for this recognition, and the employee gets a 22squared plastic clapper. It's kind of silly, it's very inexpensive, and it works! We also just upped our game with a pin that is "flair" these employees can display similar to the stickers placed on the back of football players' helmets after key plays.

We also give our employees coupons to redeem for merchandise from our 22squared store when they hit milestones. We've done our best to stock the store with items they'll actually use—like water bottles that keep drinks chilled for 24 hours, and umbrellas. And every year, we give everyone on the team our annual company T-shirt. This isn't just any old boxy cotton T. It's specially designed and made out of high-quality, breathable material so our employees will want to wear it around town. If your employees aren't proud enough to put a sticker of your firm on their laptop or wear the T-shirt, then you may want to rethink your brand. ;)

Here are three photos of our Swag Room at 22squared:

QUICK SUMMARY

- Investing in your employees is a great way to build their loyalty and willingness to go the extra mile for you. Putting money into tools and training that equip your Millennial team members to do their jobs better can absolutely transform their job performance.
- It's important to recognize your employees because it makes them happier. Happiness increases the potential, productivity, and loyalty of your employees.

- If an employee can't be trusted to get work done then they shouldn't be on your team. If they want to work from home trust them to get the work done at home.
- Rewards, no matter how small, can encourage employees to go that extra mile.

MAKE IT HAPPEN.

1. Use the awards you give your employees as an opportunity to build brand loyalty. Let your team be proud to display your bumper sticker on their cars and to wear your T-shirt.
2. Make sure that even if a department leader isn't heavy on recognition, there are fail-safes that give people opportunities to be recognized.
3. Invest in training that will lead to long-term performance improvements in your team, and remember that things like mindfulness, meditation, and yoga can be just as helpful as another sales or marketing training.
4. Have awards at the ready to recognize people unexpectedly.
5. Set a budget for creative team bonding.
6. Force your workforce to unplug in order to unwind.
7. Train your Millennial team members to answer their "Let's" with a "By when?" to bring accountability to their statements and ideas.
8. Make sure that you are personally accessible to each one of your team members. They should be able to reach you nearly constantly. Most of them won't try to, but the fact that they know they can will make an enormous difference in morale.

9. Slow your team down to speed them up! For specific strategies on how to do this, I've compiled a resource packet that will show you how. Grab it at TheMillennialWhisperer.com/BookResources

CHAPTER 7

PROMOTING MILLENNIALS

Motivating Them to Advance up the Corporate Ladder

If you're not promoted every year, you're a failure. This is how most high-achieving Millennials feel. And most corporate cultures foster this unattainable belief.

Let's consider the case of Meg Roberts, who came to 22squared from a traditional company with a bi-annual promotion calendar: every April and October, top-performing employees received promotions. Those who didn't felt unvalued, unmotivated, and uninspired. Worse, they considered their work output to be below average, leading to a cycle of decreasing productivity and quality until, eventually, they left. The company suffered from high turnover and low morale as well as a deep organizational chart. But, even for those getting the promotions, there can be negative impact: what happens when you feel like you already know the reward you'll receive year after year? Meg felt unchallenged and unfilled, so she left the company.

When I started managing Meg, we had an in-depth and transparent conversation about her goals and passions. I urged her to think beyond a promotion: what did she really want to be doing that would leave her motivated and fulfilled?

She expressed interest in managing people, and not just to add to her resume or because she felt she needed to have direct reports to move to the next level. Her passions for people and the work collided as she talked about wanting to help develop other team members' skill sets based on their strengths. She genuinely wanted to coach people in order to make our work better.

Together, we worked on a tailored development grid that allowed her to focus on her day-to-day responsibilities and technical skills while also giving her room to develop her coaching and leadership.

Meg has now been at 22squared for five years, more than twice the time she'd been at any other company previously.

"What Motivates You?"

In previous chapters we touched on how Millennials don't necessarily desire a traditional path to promotion. For this generation, it's much more about *progression* than *promotion*. Remember the question Ad Tech Executive Meredith Guerriero asks each new hire: "What motivates you?"

Knowing the answer to that question helps Meredith craft a promotional path for her team members that will help them achieve their own personal goals *while* serving the company well. She has this great analogy about a rocket ship. As long as people are on her team, they're building *the company's* rocket ship. It's a team effort that serves a common purpose. She serves as an inspirational leader to all of her recruits so they stay focused on the big purpose behind the company's goals.

To ensure that all team members are aware of their place on that rocket ship, Meredith gives regular feedback *in real time* and clearly communicates company standards. The key is giving people a heads up on how they can both meet their own personal goals *and* bolster the company's bottom line. Meredith builds that in through a constant feedback loop that builds trust and transparency.

Toppling Tradition

For decades, the gold standard of corporate life was earning your pension and your gold watch and retiring after 25 years of service. Respected. Honored. Appreciated.

That culture doesn't exist anymore. We all saw how ruthlessly companies cut employees who'd spent their whole lives serving when the 2008 recession rolled through. And whereas Baby Boomers used to get and keep a job for more than 20 years on average, stats from the Bureau of Labor Statistics show that the average worker these days holds ten different positions before the age of 40.

Traditions are toppling, even in time-honored professions like law. Before the recession, young associates accepted that they'd have to sweat it out with early mornings, late nights, and packed weekends at prestigious law firm. But the light at the end of that eight-year tunnel was making partner—with its commensurate pay increase and workload decrease.

That changed after 2008. Many clients tightened their belts and quit paying for travel and administrative expenses. They expected more work for less pay, and firms followed suit, requiring more work to make partner and offering fewer perks. As a result, Millennial lawyers have pushed back. There's a whole new crew of attorneys with zero desire to make partner. They want to do interesting, purposeful work without completely sacrificing family time, and they're willing to accept a fraction of the traditional lawyer pay to have that work-life integration.

Firms benefit from this new progression path, too. In the past, the legal path was "up or out." If an associate didn't make partner after nine years, he or she was generally put out to pasture. Nearly a decade of training and investment went to waste.

Now, by embracing Millennials' own desires for work-life integration, firms get the benefit of retaining top talent without having to give partner-sized paychecks. Everybody wins.

More and more companies are seeing that they get more from their Millennial employees by tailoring progression plans that meet their employees' stated desires. And Millennials generally desire quick feedback and wins. One study showed that 40% of Millennials expect a promotion every one to two years, and they desire raises, promotions, and bonuses more than once a year. This generation also *expects* things that were perks to older generations—like offices with doors that shut as opposed to cubicles, which have no doors.

I do think one stereotype that is true is that Millennials feel they should be constantly promoted . . . it's exhausting, I know. One of the key things 22squared did to address this was to create distinct development grids that employees are taken through periodically to address their current job, its actual responsibilities . . . how they're performing in each of these areas, and then compare it to a grid for the job that they think they already deserve. This approach clearly outlines where the employee still needs to develop in their current role and where the future responsibilities lie. One of the best things my boss Brandon instilled in me was to start doing the job you think you deserve first, so promotion is a no-brainer by the time you're considered for it because you're already doing it.

You can download a sample development grid you can customize and use in your company on the Resources page (TheMillennialWhisperer. com/BookResources).

Many Touchpoints

To give Millennials the amount of feedback and direction they desire (and require in order to perform at their highest levels), it's likely going to feel like you're overcommunicating. We've tried to systematize this at 22squared by using a development grid showing each employee's current job title and the one he or she would be promoted into next. We communicate clearly where they stand in that grid so that they know exactly where they need to improve in order to reach their desired position.

Choose Your Own Adventure

Allowing Millennials to pursue their passions within their current roles can also help them stay engaged between promotional periods. It's helpful to let go of the linear thinking we used to embrace regarding jobs and positions and instead help each key team member craft his or her own custom path.

As Pete Cashmore, the founder of Mashable, says: "It comes down to the individual person. The best organizations figure out how to combine the experience of their more senior employees with the zeal and ability to adapt quickly of the Millennials."

I like to use the analogy of an ant farm. Every single ant matters. Each one has a role to play. But they aren't all going straight to the queen. Some are worker ants who scurry side to side for their entire lives. They still play a vital part in the health of the colony. But the path must feel open to constant adjustments and turns instead of something that has been set out in front of these Millennials. Your company will stand out from the competition when you allow Millennials to choose their own path. Remember that within an ant farm, there is still structure. Provide clear job descriptions and outlines to your team members so they can make an informed decision on whether they actually desire to move into a specific role.

If you're in a more traditional industry where it's still expected that there's a clear climb up the ranks, consider building two different promotional tracks into your corporate structure: one traditional and one that promotes people for being individual contributors.

Millennials don't thrive in the one-track-up environment. Many of them don't want to move up to management. If that's the case, giving them a promotion that removes them from doing what they love could have the opposite effect. They might want to progress by being given more autonomy or time to engage in special projects. There needs to be a different track. This can be as simple as asking your best performers what their goals are once they've been with you long enough to have these types of conversations.

The companies that have been able to incorporate creative promotional paths have had great success in the modern economy. Facebook, The Honest Company, Pinterest . . . the list goes on of companies that have leveraged their Millennial employees' creativity to build new business opportunities. For example, Mary Katherine Rordam now leads our Influencer Marketing Department, a profitable team of more than 10 people that was born out of a creative approach she brought to a campaign idea in 2011. Our concept for The Costa Rica Tourism Board involved using one-third of the marketing budget to send people on free trips to the country. Mary Katherine was tasked with helping with PR for the campaign but suggested we customize a portion of the free trips for influencers who could create content on our behalf. After the success of that campaign, she built out our Influencer Marketing offering, and now partners with hundreds of influencers each year on behalf of our different clients.

QUICK SUMMARY

- Millennials expect promotions. Most high-achieving Millennials feel that if they're not promoted in a year, then they're a failure.
  - What's the solution?

- For decades, the gold standard of corporate life was earning your pension and your gold watch and retiring after 25 years of service. That culture doesn't exist anymore.
  - What does this mean for leaders?

MAKE IT HAPPEN.

1. Give Millennials autonomy. They need to be able to put their finger on the impact that their individual contribution is making. They need to know they're contributing to a bigger purpose before they'll give you their continued best effort.
2. Millennials long for an *inspirational* leader. We put the wrong leaders into management positions and the wrong managers into leadership positions. You need to keep your logistics / numbers person in their zone of genius—you *must* choose an inspirational leader to balance out the analytical person.
3. Millennials need to create their own path.
4. If you have a traditional hierarchical company structure, consider reworking your longevity plan. Offer more nontraditional options to keep your top team members engaged in their zones of genius.
5. Develop two "promotional" tracks: one for the traditional hierarchical structure and another that allows people to rise up the ranks as *individual* contributors.

CHAPTER 8

MAINTAINING MILLENNIAL MORALE

What to Do When Things Go Wrong or You Need to Have Difficult Conversations

Picture this: you're Liza Wood Nebel, Partner and COO at Blackbelt. ai, a Gen Xer who's spent nearly 20 years negotiating the corporate world. You essentially have a black belt in managing people with grace, compassion, and inspiration.

You have a Millennial employee (we'll call her Madison) who is smart, motivated, accomplished. She has come from nothing, and you've been empowering her at Blackbelt.ai. But then she starts making errors, and more errors.

One day, Madison goes to lunch with employees from a competing company, and comes back to the office drunk.

You send her home. The next day, Madison says she can't come into work—she's been sick from bad sushi, she says, and she has an important yoga class to attend at 5:30.

(Yes, this is a true story. I couldn't possibly make this up.)

You send a calendar invite for a feedback session. Madison calls immediately and says, "I'm going to quit; you don't need to fire me."

Huh?

"We weren't going to fire you; would you like to have a feedback session Friday?"

Madison says no.

Double huh?

It's a true story of some of the "extreme" behaviors, as Liza says, her firm experiences from Millennials.

So, how do we handle such behaviors?

The answer is surprising. (And no, not as in surprising Madison with a bunch of note-filled balloons. I'm sentimental, not stupid.)

Mastering the Art of the Graceful Release

If I haven't made it abundantly clear already, I wrote this book to prove that there are plenty of awesome Millennials in the job pool who will make excellent long-term employees for your organization. When you build a Millennial-friendly culture, align your younger workers' job duties with their passions, and then provide them with inspirational leadership alongside autonomy, they will surprise you with their loyalty and willingness to go the extra mile.

However, all of us have made bad hires. The key in correcting a misaligned hiring decision is to let that employee go quickly—I call it the "graceful release."

Negativity is extremely damaging to the workplace. Failing to proactively maintain a culture of positivity will disrupt employee engagement and productivity. On a minor scale, negativity can be found in gossip, attitude, and general communication. But it can evolve into more severe situations such as harassment. The US Bureau of Labor

Statistics has reported that negativity costs businesses $3 billion a year due to its harmful effects.

Zappos CEO Tony Hsieh once estimated bad hires had cost the company well over $100 million. According to the US Department of Labor, the price of a bad hire is at least 30% of the employee's first year earnings.

I spoke with a young lawyer whose next-door officemate was incredibly negative. She complained about everything and everyone. She'd also slip out for several hours during the day and refused to stay late or work weekends (even when the team really needed her). Yet everyone knew this worker was being compensated at a senior level. It was devastating to morale.

Eventually, this team member *did* get terminated (but far too late). The lawyer who had the burden of working next door to her didn't realize how negatively her own work had been impacted until that negative attorney was gone. Her new office neighbor was positive, and it was like a dark cloud had lifted from the entire office floor.

For the sake of your team's morale, let any "problem children" go quickly and compassionately. If possible, help them relocate to a company or position that's a better fit. Let your employees see that you protect the integrity of the team by removing anyone who's misplaced. Remember that your entire team is watching to see if you'll stick up for the good of the whole.

Also, don't forget "protect this house." Empower your workforce to self-police and hold up the standards for the rest of the group. When someone doesn't meet the group's expectations, they'll feel that and will either self-correct or self-select out.

Real-Time Reviews

There's one phrase on a whiteboard that everyone in our department walks by. It says, "Every day is a performance review in this department."

It's important to me that I give my team consistent and real-time feedback. I remember when I was 26 years old and went into my review as a copywriter. I had been working the job for four months, and looking back, I can see that my work was likely subpar. But I had never been reviewed before. I was just chugging along churning out online demo work.

My review was horrendous. I was so blindsided and upset that I stormed out of the office, got in my car, called the CEO, and told him he'd better find me a new department to move into. It's how I got out of the Creative Department into another department around trendspotting and social media. I will never forget that moment of feeling totally humiliated and caught off guard.

Waiting too long to give necessary feedback can destroy your team morale and have your employees hunting for new jobs.

Contrast that experience with the work I did once I moved into the New Business Department at 22squared. Christy Cross (who now leads Business Development) gave us feedback at the end of each practice speech as well as after any big presentation. We could see her pen clicking away during our presentations, and just knew it would be something critical. She was brutal. "You said 'um' five times and 'like' 15 times. You stumbled on your words and this point fell short. Also, your answer to the client's first question was long-winded."

But because the feedback was given in real time, it only stung for a minute. Then we learned from it and moved on.

Feedback and "Nose Flicks" as New Ways to Measure Progress

What else can we do to counteract how a lifetime of consistent praise and trophies has caused an entire generation to expect promotions every three months?

We could take a page out of Meredith Guerriero's playbook at Pinterest and focus on feedback and what she calls the "nose flicks" of constructive criticism. Remember, Millennials aren't entitled. They just grew up constantly praised and rewarded. If we spend our time pushing back and complaining about that reality, we'll make our lives much harder and create conflict where there doesn't need to be any.

Hiding constructive feedback for fear that we'll "lose" the Millennials can build resentment and lead to a culture that accepts anything less than excellent work. That can reflect poorly on our companies and cause us to lose clients or build a bad reputation in the industry.

So, keeping feedback to ourselves until the review period isn't a good option. Plus, waiting for those scheduled review periods before giving feedback can hit Millennials hard, seemingly coming out of nowhere. (That's true with all employees, really.)

To avoid this and build a culture of transparency and consistent improvement, Meredith focuses on consistent feedback and "nose flicks" instead of letting things build up to what can feel like a quarterly gut punch. She makes sure all employees know the expectations are high and everyone (including Meredith) needs to focus on consistent improvement. And she lets them know she's committed to helping them do that by pointing out areas of improvement in real time, which are what she means by "nose flicks."

Her team members know there's no quarterly promotion or annual advancement guarantee. They also know expectations go up as they get better and promotion and recognition come from meeting expectations.

While this sounds like it could create friction between her and her team members, it generally has the opposite effect. Employees know exactly how they're performing and what to improve upon. They also know the "nose flicks" aren't a signal to polish up their résumés but are instead constructive feedback to help the team succeed together.

She's created a culture of real-time feedback, where no one person feels singled out because everyone (including Meredith) is focused on consistent improvement. Everyone gets nose flicks. It's just the company culture of letting people know how they can improve; it's not a personal attack. If and when they learn from the feedback and improve, they earn the appropriate recognition or promotion, no preset promotion schedule required.

A Better Sandwich

Sandwiching criticism between positive feedback can help your Millennial employees integrate your instructions into the way they perform their jobs more easily. Paying a compliment first will set your employee at ease and let him know that his job isn't at risk when you then point out how he can improve. Then after you've given the piece of criticism, tack on one more positive affirmation so the conversation ends on a high note.

Giving feedback in real time, as we've repeatedly discussed in this book, also softens the blow of any negative feedback. We give mini-reviews at 22squared on a consistent basis, and pretty much every Millennial leader I interviewed for this book has some way of giving a performance assessment at least quarterly.

One final note is that most of the criticism we give is in private while the praise is public. This creates an atmosphere where our Millennials feel safe and protected. They'll go to bat for us because they trust that even if they mess up, they remain part of a valued team, and that we'll still have their back.

Oh, Behave!

Now, let's return to Liza Wood Nebel at Blackbet.ai. She focuses on retaining and nurturing Millennial talent in an environment where a lot of corporate "flirting" goes on: San Francisco. Opportunities there are plentiful. It's low-risk for employees to move to new companies, but high-cost for employers to replace them.

To combat this "greener grass" perception that some Millennials hold, Liza is focused on aligning her hiring choices with what she can offer her Millennial employees. Blackbelt.ai is specifically looking for people who are hungry to learn and who desire to make jumps in their career quickly. They want people who are ready to prove something, who can move at the pace of innovation, and who don't shy away from ambiguity.

They also recognize the strong pull to flirt around at many companies as a way for potential hires to meet these types of personal objectives. Liza recognizes her Millennial employees' desire to move around every 18 months as a way to broaden their skillset, network, and gain exposure to new thinking.

She's very clear about a strong asset Blackbelt.ai has that some others do not: thriving local partnerships with technology and talent networks that every employee is encouraged to tap into. Coupled with the emotional drivers of her employee base and the actual assets the company has in place, her approach to talent growth and retention has been to put something called "cross training" in place. Part of each person's performance-management plan is to allow them to pick a completely separate functional discipline and to train in it—both formally through *paid* training and also through informal mentorship from others within the organization or network.

As an example, Liza will allow a data scientist who wants to become a better storyteller to shadow a creative lead, spend time in an off-site storytelling program for advertisers, or bring his new skill set into the data-science presentations that sometimes can fall flat for people who don't love or understand complex algorithms, modeling in R, and coding in Python.

The result is that Blackbelt.ai's employees have been able to explore something else they have interest in without leaving the company. (Unless, ahem, they leave for lunch and return tipsy. Nice one, Madison.) The company has further benefited from having a few people who've trained in other disciplines long enough to have a skill set that makes them viable for other types of client work.

These actions help Liza retain employees who are happy, engaged, and in pursuit of knowledge that complements Blackbelt.ai's culture, while also giving her the flexibility to have the resources she needs to deploy on project work versus having to outsource or turn work away. This is both a cultural *and* a financial win for the company.

QUICK SUMMARY

- Hire slow and fire fast. All of us have made bad hires. Make a "graceful release." Negativity is extremely damaging to the workplace.
- Give your employees "nose flicks" rather than quarterly gut punches. Create a culture of real-time feedback.
- Build a "better sandwich" so that you can provide criticism to employees more effectively and politely.

—— MAKE IT HAPPEN. ——

1. Things go wrong in business. People quit or need to be let go. There will be times when you've got to cut a Millennial loose. Do it as quickly and gracefully as possible.

2. Make sure you discipline *in the moment*. Millennials are conditioned to expect a nearly instantaneous feedback loop, so it's important that you don't let issues linger.

3. When you do give feedback on something a Millennial team member did that did not meet your expectations, make sure that you are giving that feedback from a place of compassion. Avoid all hints of a hierarchical or condescending tone.

4. Make sure to keep your criticism private, and make your rewards public (See Chapter 5 on how to reward and recognize your Millennial team members).

5. Sandwich any criticism with compliments. Always give feedback pursuant to this formula: positive contribution + critique + positive contribution. Be as authentically optimistic as you reasonably can.

6. Regularly engage in mini-reviews. The worst thing you can do with a Millennial is to wait an entire year to give feedback. Reviews should happen quarterly at a minimum, with more casual feedback being offered in the moment as needed (see point # 2).

7. Remember that your entire team is watching how you treat other team members. One bad apple left to rot will spoil the whole barrel. Your team will respect you more for calling out bad behavior quickly, while it can still be addressed without destroying office morale.

8. Where possible, if you must release a team member, help that person find work that is a better fit for him or her.

MAKE IT HAPPEN

A Millennial, a Gen Xer, and a Baby Boomer walk into a bar.

The bartender looks up and says, "Is this some kind of a joke?"

Let's admit it, together: we have misunderstood and mismanaged Millennials for too long. And we have all suffered. Millennials have suffered. Businesses have suffered. And our clients and customers have suffered.

When I returned from my month-long sabbatical, 22squared put me in charge of a small team of Millennials and a department considered an "investment" rather than a profit center. The strategies I've shared with you in this book helped me reverse that in short order.

These strategies can help you, too, no matter what you have for a budget or what level of your leadership you have at your company.

If you have to start small, start small.

But just start.

And keep going.

Because soon enough, you'll see signs that you, too, are on your way to becoming a Millennial Whisperer.

At first, the signs may be small. You see that you've saved a measurable amount of money by eliminating things that don't matter to your Millennial team members. You feel a noticeable positive energy boost in your team, department, or across the company. You observe an obvious shift in how your team members interact with each other, working better together and supporting each other well. But be patient with yourself and expect pushback as the results will *not* come overnight.

Leading with inspiration and empathy while also understanding the drive and purpose behind your Millennial team members does not mean you're losing sight of the business at hand . . . you just have to be a bit patient to let it blossom out of your people as the culture and drive shifts. The profitability *will* follow.

Over time, these small shifts will add up, and you will see even bigger signs and better results.

How to Know You're Heading in the Right Direction

You can look for three distinct areas of impact to know that you're implementing these strategies effectively.

- Things that are measurable (such as costs, productivity, turnover, profits)
- Things you can feel (such as energy and excitement)
- Things you can observe (such as people working well together, going to lunch together, hanging out together outside of work, and participating in charity events together)

How to Know You've Become a Millennial Whisperer

You're scrolling through images of cats and sunset cocktails on Instagram when you see it: a post from your company, with a hashtag that shows Millennial pride in your workplace.

Or you see Millennials wearing your company shirt or putting your company's bumper sticker on their car.

Bingo. You've become a Millennial Whisperer.

You Got This

Your team may not be ready to tattoo your logo on their back. But they crave *inspiration*, *transparency*, and *autonomy within structure*. They need us to create a culture and provide the structure for them to thrive.

And when they succeed, we succeed.

So we, as leaders, must set ourselves up to succeed in leading the biggest, most resourceful, and most passionate generation in history. To do that, we must *implement* the strategies we know to move us forward.

Maybe it's pushing it a bit too far to preorder a stack of logo tattoo stencils right now. But it's not too far to start to implement the things we need to do to become Millennial Whisperers.

And while a great leader never blames her tools if something goes wrong, I want to help you move forward by giving you some of the best tools and resources I know (and use) to help me lead my team of Millennials.

Visit the Resources page at TheMillennialWhisperer.com/BookResources. Be sure to bookmark that page because we'll be updating it with new stories and additional resources.

There, you can download free tools, templates, meeting agendas, and more. Many of those forms are the exact ones we use at 22squared to recruit, hire, and motivate our amazing team of Millennials.

You will also find success stories and case studies of other companies who have found their own *Millennial Whisperers*. You can also submit your own success story or Millennial Whisperer strategy to potentially be featured on the site and help your fellow leaders.

Also, if you haven't yet taken the free Millennial Leadership Assessment, you can find that on the Resources page. We partnered with G360 Talent Development to build a custom Millennial Leadership Assessment to allow you to analyze your strengths or identify areas for improvement in leading Millennials.

The assessment is based on the best and latest research on Millennials in the workplace and built from the ground up by the G360 Talent Development team led Dr. Brian Griffith, a professor, author, and former director of the Human and Organizational Development Program at Vanderbilt University.

And it was built just for you, so you can move one step closer to becoming the *Millennial Whisperer* in your organization.

I hope the Millennial Leadership Assessment, along with the tools, resources, and the words in this book, resonate with you and call you to take action to make things easier and better for your company, your team, and you.

I hope you implement these ideas and reach out to me to share your *Millennial Whisperer* stories. Use the tools on the Resources page to help you out. There's no reason to reinvent the wheel if you don't have to.

Finally, I've created a closed Facebook group exclusively for readers of *The Millennial Whisperer* to connect, share stories, and support each other as we all work to become better leaders. It's a group by leaders, of leaders, and for leaders of the greatest generation to enter the workforce in modern history. Harness the power of community and join me and other Millennial Whisperers at TheMillennialWhisperer.com/ Community.

So, while this is the conclusion of *The Millennial Whisperer*, the book, it's just the beginning of our never-ending discussion of how we can be passionate (without suffering from a passion disorder) about blending generations to create one heckuva productive workplace, and world.

Let's turn these whispers into a bigger conversation.

Take The Millennial Leadership Assessment and Get Resources and Implementation Materials to Become a Millennial Whisperer at:

TheMillennialWhisperer.com/BookResources

ABOUT THE AUTHOR

Chris Tuff is a partner at the advertising agency 22squared in Atlanta, where he took a team of Millennials from an "investment" to a major profit center in short order.

Chris started his career as one of the first marketers to focus on helping startups work with Fortune 100 brands, including Facebook in 2005.

Since then, he's become a sought-after leader in the digital marketing space and

Photo credit: Uchechi Anusiem

has been featured on the front page of the *Wall Street Journal*, in *Fast Company*, and consistently in advertising trade publication features, including *Ad Age* and *Advertising Weekly*.

When Chris isn't working, he kiteboards, mountain bikes, runs, and spends quality time with his wife and two daughters.

You can contact Chris on Twitter @christuff.

ENDNOTES

Introduction

1   Richard Fry, "Pew Research Fact Tank," "Millennials Are the Largest Generation in the US Labor Force" http://www.pewresearch.org/fact-tank/2018/04/11/millennials-largest-generation-us-labor-force/

2   "Google Support," https://support.google.com/websearch/answer/106230?co=GENIE.Platform%3DAndroid&hl=en

3   Ibid.

4   Christine Elliot and William Reynolds, *The Atlantic*, https://www.theatlantic.com/sponsored/deloitte-shifts/making-it-millennial/259/

5   Ibid.

6   IBM Institute for Business Value, "Myths, Exaggerations, and Uncomfortable Truths" ftp://ftp.software.ibm.com/software//nz/downloads/Myths_exaggerations_and_uncomfortable_truths_Executive_Report.pdf

7   Deloitte Global, The Deloitte Millennial Survey 2018, May 2018, (https://www2.deloitte.com/content/dam/Deloitte/global/Documents/About-Deloitte/gx-2018-millennial-survey-report.pdf)

8   Patagonia https://www.patagonia.com/company-info.html

Chapter 3

9   Deloitte Global, The Deloitte Millennial Survey 2017, January 2017, (https://www2.deloitte.com/content/dam/Deloitte/

global/Documents/About-Deloitte/gx-deloitte-millennial-survey-2017-executive-summary.pdf)

10 Deloitte Global, The Deloitte Millennial Innovation Survey 2013, January 2013, (https://www2.deloitte.com/content/dam/Deloitte/global/Documents/About-Deloitte/dttl-millennial-innovation-survey.pdf)

11 Deloitte Global, The Deloitte Millennial Survey 2018, May 2018, (https://www2.deloitte.com/content/dam/Deloitte/global/Documents/About-Deloitte/gx-2018-millennial-survey-report.pdf)

12 Gallup, "Gallup Daily," "U.S. Employee Engagement," https://news.gallup.com/poll/180404/gallup-daily-employee-engagement.aspx

13 Brian Brim, "Gallup Daily," "Do Your Teams Own Their Engagement?" https://www.gallup.com/workplace/242054/teams-own-engagement.aspx

14 Ibid.

15 AON, "Employee Engagement Rebounds To Match All-Time High" http://www.aon.com/2018-global-employee-engagement-trends/index.html

16 Cigna, "New Cigna Study Reveals Loneliness At Epidemic Levels In America"

17 University of Pittsburgh Schools of Health Sciences, "More Social Connection Online Tied to Increasing Feelings of Isolation" https://www.eurekalert.org/pub_releases/2017-03/uops-msc022817.php

18 Caroline Barton, "Forbes," "Why Millennials Are Lonely" https://www.forbes.com/sites/carolinebeaton/2017/02/09/why-millennials-are-lonely/#284268907c35

19 Aaron Smith and Monica Anderson, "Pew Research Center," "Social Media Use in 2018" http://www.pewinternet. org/2018/03/01/social-media-use-in-2018/

20 Leslie Haddon, "Semantic Scholar," "Social Media and Youth" https://pdfs.semanticscholar.org/ d439/557c9ed0340fb5169f271efe320f39493d75.pdf

21 Jean M. Twenge, Thomas E. Joiner, Megan L. Rogers, and Gabrielle N. Martin; "Association for Psychological Science" Increases in Depressive Symptoms, Suicide-Related Outcomes, and Suicide Rates Among U.S. Adolescents After 2010 and Links to Increased New Media Screen Time" https://www. avaate.org/IMG/pdf/suicidio2167702617723376.pdf

Chapter 4

22 https://nypost.com/2017/11/14/rise-in-teen-suicide-connected-to-social-media-popularity-study/

23 "New York Post," "Rise in Teen Suicide Conncted to Social Media Popularity: Study" https://nypost.com/2017/11/14/rise-in-teen-suicide-connected-to-social-media-popularity-study/

24 Bentley University, "The Millennial Mind Goes to Work" https://www.bentley.edu/newsroom/latest-headlines/mind-of-millennial

Chapter 6

25 Eliza Kuhner, "Wired," "Why It's So Hard to Be a Working Mom. Even at Facebook." https://www.wired.com/story/i-am-a-data-scientist-and-mom-but-facebook-made-me-choose/

Morgan James makes all of our titles available
through the Library for All Charity Organization.

www.LibraryForAll.org